CAR
MARQUES

A Graphic Guide to Automotive Logos and Emblems

Brimming with creative inspiration, how-to projects, and useful information to enrich your everyday life, Quarto Knows is a favourite destination for those pursuing their interests and passions. Visit our site and dig deeper with our books into your area of interest: Quarto Creates, Quarto Cooks, Quarto Homes, Quarto Lives, Quarto Drives, Quarto Explores, Quarto Gifts, or Quarto Kids.

Inspiring | Educating | Creating | Entertaining

Conceived, Designed and Produced by Quintet Publishing, an imprint of The Quarto Group
The Old Brewery, 6 Blundell Street, London N7 9BH, United Kingdom
T (0)20 7700 6700 **F** (0)20 7700 8066 **www.QuartoKnows.com**

First published in 2018 by Motorbooks, an imprint of The Quarto Group,
401 Second Avenue North, Suite 310, Minneapolis, MN 55401 USA.
T (612) 344-8100 F (612) 344-8692 www.QuartoKnows.com

Motorbooks titles are also available at discount for retail, wholesale, promotional, and bulk purchase. For details, contact the Special Sales Manager by email at specialsales@quarto.com or by mail at The Quarto Group, Attn: Special Sales Manager, 401 Second Avenue North, Suite 310, Minneapolis, MN 55401 USA.

10 9 8 7 6 5 4 3 2 1

ISBN: 978-0-7603-6245-7

Digital edition published in 2018
eISBN: 978-0-7603-6246-4

Printed in China

CAR
MARQUES

A Graphic Guide to Automotive
Logos and Emblems

Simon Heptinstall

CONTENTS

INTRODUCTION

As this book was being written, Mercedes and AMG unveiled a futuristic new supercar to the world's press. Most of the motoring journalists assembled at the 2017 Frankfurt International Motor Show event agreed that the car that was revealed, the "Project One," is an extraordinary machine.

The new Mercedes is a multimillion dollar Formula One car for the road, featuring a very similar engine to three-time world champion Lewis Hamilton's racing car. It's the sort of machine that seems completely divorced from the cars the rest of us mere mortal car enthusiasts see and drive every day. It's more like a flying saucer. Project One's high-tech, race-bred components seem to have more to do with science fiction than everyday motoring . . . apart from one.

Firmly fixed to the lightweight carbon panel forming the steeply raked aerodynamic hood of the Project One is a component shared with humble family hatchbacks, estate cars, and even tatty commercial vans across the world. It is one of the world's most familiar commercial logos: the Mercedes' three-pointed star.

This component demonstrates that even a millionaire's supercar needs to be identified. In this instance, Mercedes wants the world to know that Project One represents the same brand values and image as the humble A-Class family hatchback and the Vito panel van.

It announces to the world that this is just one of the examples of what Mercedes can produce, and that some of the company's technological magnificence is shared with the rather less technically advanced products from the same company. Someone buying a lesser product with the same badge will feel part of the "club," elevated by the prestige of the Project One supercar.

The new Mercedes owner wants everyone else to see exactly what his or her money has been spent on. The simple hood badge has helped create a brand identity that can be a major selling point.

BUILDING A BRAND IDENTITY

A car's badge may be a component that many of us rarely think about. It may be a simple stamped piece of chrome or plastic glued or plugged into place. But this vital part of a car fulfills several major functions: the car logo is part advertisement, part decoration, and part identity tag.

Identity tag? Well, everyone from marketing gurus to amateur car-spotters likes to be able to tell one car from another. The manufacturer's logo is one of the most important ways to do this, and not just for supercars. Try identifying any vehicle where the emblem and name have been lost or removed. Could you really tell one modern hatchback from another with no badge to help you? Even experienced motoring journalists can find familiar cars hard to name without their logos and company branding.

The simple, long-standing emblems and the successful companies behind them usually demonstrate how it's done. Volkswagen and Ferrari are excellent examples of this. The VW symbol is as old as its first car, the iconic Beetle, and Enzo Ferrari's famous prancing horse has adorned his cars since the birth of the company. Both companies have done rather well with a simple but unchanging brand identity. And one thing is for sure: neither of these world-famous badges is ever likely to change.

THE STORIES BEHIND THE BADGES

The stories of how these brand emblems have evolved along with the vehicles give a glimpse into how the world of marketing and design has changed over the last century.

Each badge has a different story to tell.

Some of the earliest car badges were simply the name of the owner of the company written in a script, as if the owner had personally signed the hood of his vehicles. Some have origins dating back into history, far beyond the birth of the motor car. For example, Vauxhall's griffin has its roots in the heraldic device of an English medieval knight, while the Pontiac emblems link back to a Native American chieftain who fought against the British colonialists almost three centuries ago.

Often a car manufacturer's badge has evolved through more than a century of the ideas, dreams, and skills of entrepreneurs, designers, artists, and businessmen. The Cadillac badge, for example, has been gradually refined over the last 100 years until it almost seems an abstract piece of art. This might seem in keeping with the company's premium brand image. In reality, however, the badge is a graphic simplification of the design chosen by the pioneering businessmen who established the company in 1902.

Other marques have stuttered through a sequence of wildly different badges and consequently struggled to build a brand identity. Perhaps the Oldsmobile marque may have prospered a little longer if it hadn't confused customers by switching between florid crests, winged spurs, ringed globes, and space rockets.

ABOUT THIS BOOK

This book is a great way to discover and understand the world of car badges. It's a collection of the best-known, most common, and most interesting motoring emblems. More than 90 badges of motoring marques, both current and defunct, are examined in detail. They range from the simple, such as Jeep or MG, to the elaborate, like Alfa Romeo or Porsche.

The combination of color illustrations and black-and-white line art provides a fascinating chance to see the badges isolated from the cars to appreciate the design and marketing concepts behind them. Insightful annotations are provided for the line-art version of the badges, picking out the details that make each badge unique and that are relevant to the origins of the brand. Beneath each badge, the key colors are indicated with swatches that provide both the CMYK color breakdown for print specification, and the closest possible match to the relevant hex code for on-screen use in websites.

The details of the badges sometimes reveal intimate details about how a company works: Aston Martin's winged badge, for example, is handmade by jewelers in the heart of the city of

Birmingham, England, while one of the world's most expensive car brands, Koenigsegg, uses a badge that was designed by the founder's school friend.

In addition, the book offers a chance to read about the stories behind these extraordinary badges, such as the famous Rolls-Royce "Spirit of Ecstasy" hood figurine, the flamboyant emblem that was modeled on the secret lover of a motoring-mad aristocrat.

Sprinkled among the badges are two types of feature spread. The first shows the historical evolution of certain badges, including Cadillac, Fiat, and Vauxhall. The second profiles some of the great figures of the car world, figures who shaped the automotive industry and also had a hand in the design of some iconic car badges.

THE BADGES

ABARTH

FOUNDED
March 31 1949 (Bologna, Italy)

FOUNDER(S)
Carlo Abarth

YEARS OF OPERATION
1949–present

BEST-KNOWN MODELS
Fiat-Abarth 500, Abarth 595, Abarth 124 Spider

Our first marque is arguably one of the most striking. Abarth was founded by the Austrian-Italian engineer and designer Carlo Abarth. Abarth had previously been involved in motorsports, particularly motorcycle racing, in which he won five European Championship titles, until serious accidents in 1930 and 1939 forced his retirement from the sport. After starting out as a racing team that developed parts for production cars, the company relocated to Turin, Italy in April 1951, where its long-running relationship with Fiat began.

The fierce scorpion emblem which provides the principal feature for the marque was chosen by Abarth himself as it is his zodiacal birth sign (he was born in November 1908). The story goes that Abarth also felt it was an ugly creature that wouldn't be intimidated by other marques, an appropriate quality considering the company's close association with the world of automobile racing.

The shield emblem, a common component of car marque design, represents both prestige and victory, while the red and yellow halves represent the energy and passion behind the design of the cars. Finally, the Italian flag is represented by three green, white, and red stripes below the company's name in the top portion of the shield. Although he was born in Austria, Abarth was extremely passionate about the strong automotive heritage entrenched in Italian culture.

The company is now a fully owned subsidiary of Fiat Chrysler Automobiles after being sold to Fiat in August 1971.

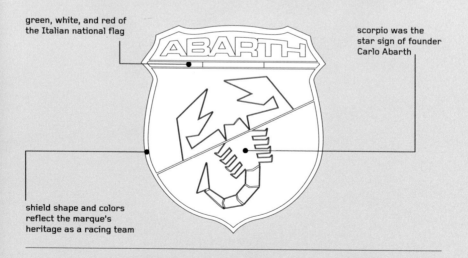

green, white, and red of
the Italian national flag

scorpio was the
star sign of founder
Carlo Abarth

shield shape and colors
reflect the marque's
heritage as a racing team

000.010.100.000
#FFE600

000.100.100.000
#FF0000

100.000.080.020
#00CC29

000.000.000.100
#000000

AC

FOUNDED
1904 (London, UK)

FOUNDER(S)
John Weller and John Portwine

YEARS OF OPERATION
1904–present

BEST-KNOWN MODELS
Cobra, Ace

One of Britain's oldest independent carmakers was named Autocar and Accessories Ltd. in 1904. However, by the 1920s, this less catchy name was shortened to AC Cars Ltd.

The marque's badge for the new, abbreviated name was a roundel containing the two initials set in an art nouveau style. Originally, there was a small hyphen between the letters. Apart from that, however, over the decades the AC badge has seen few changes. On some cars, it has appeared as two chrome capital letters with no background, while on others, the letters are featured on roundels that can be blue or black.

For 50 years the company turned out cars that have largely been forgotten, including invalid carriages and sedans with wooden frames. That changed in 1953 when engineer John Tojeiro drew up a low-slung, lightweight, open-top two-seater called the Ace. The AC Ace evolved into the even more powerful AC Cobra after American racer Carroll Shelby fitted a batch with Ford V8 engines. This legendary sports car still has a cult following today.

A Cobra was road-tested at 185 mph (295 kph) on a British freeway in 1964. Allegedly the resulting publicity was one of the reasons for the introduction of the 70 mph (110 kph) speed limit that still exists in the UK today.

Shelby's Cobra became a separate model in its own right in the USA, and wears a distinctive badge featuring a snake's head. Today's AC badge, meanwhile, retains the traditional two letters on a blue roundel, demonstrating the difference between the two markets.

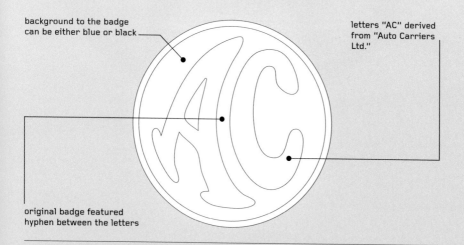

background to the badge can be either blue or black

letters "AC" derived from "Auto Carriers Ltd."

original badge featured hyphen between the letters

000.000.000.030
#B3B3B3

100.060.035.025
#004D7C

ACURA

FOUNDED
March 27 1986 (Tokyo, Japan)

FOUNDER(S)
Soichiro Honda

YEARS OF OPERATION
1986–present

BEST-KNOWN MODELS
NSX, Legend, Integra, MDX, TL

In the 1980s, Japanese motoring marques tried to heighten their appeal to the lucrative American market by devising upscale, accessible brand names. Acura was created in 1986 to serve as the luxury sub-brand of Honda. A special team at the San Francisco-based consultancy NameLab had carefully devised the name "Acura." The prefix "acu" implies accurate or precise, and matched the new brand's slogan: "Precision-crafted performance." This lofty claim to superlative and meticulous engineering seemed to fit with Acura's luxurious Legend and the supercar NSX.

Of course, the new brand came with a new logo. The Acura badge is like a futuristic letter "A" within a squashed circle. The design is simple with sharply defined line work. It bears a striking similarity to the parent company Honda's logo, which shows an "H" within a squashed square, so much so that some people thought that the Acura badge depicted a distorted 'H'. There are other ways of deciphering the Acura badge, however. Honda claims it represents an upright pair of design engineer's calipers, a device with hinged legs like a compass, used to make very accurate measurements when producing engineering drawings.

The initial batch of badges for Acura was missing the tiny horizontal bar joining the two uprights. Company head Soichiro Honda ordered the immediate recall of these, and the first batch of new cars had to have their badges prized off and replaced with the slightly adjusted logo.

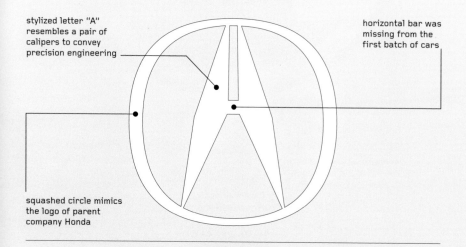

stylized letter "A" resembles a pair of calipers to convey precision engineering

horizontal bar was missing from the first batch of cars

squashed circle mimics the logo of parent company Honda

000.000.000.030
#B3B3B3

AIXAM

FOUNDED
1983 (Aix-les-Bains, France)

FOUNDER(S)
Groupe Beneteau

YEARS OF OPERATION
1983–present

BEST-KNOWN MODELS
400, Crossline

The tricolor palette of the Aixam badge demonstrates that the company's roots are firmly in the red, white, and blue of France. The very name of the marque refers to its headquarters in the city of Aix-Les-Bains in the Alpine region of Savoie.

The company emerged in 1983 but has roots dating back further. The Aixam company had bought an older operation, called Arola, which made single-seater microcars so small they could be driven without a license. Aixam took this idea and developed it, creating microvans and light utilities vehicles, plus an appealing range of small city cars. Some can still be driven without a license in some countries and Aixam claims to be the leading license-free motor manufacturer in Europe. The company is now part of a multinational American-based group. It currently offers a range of diminutive diesel, gas, and electric vehicles.

Dedicated car-spotters may notice a few variations in contemporary Aixam badging. On the nose of the latest Crossline models the Aixam word appears superimposed on the 'A' within the roundel, while on some other Aixam vehicles the logo is simply chrome with no background at all. On company materials, however, the logo usually comprises a white capital "A" with the word "Aixam" underneath it. The capital "A" usually sits in a blue roundel with a white-and-red border.

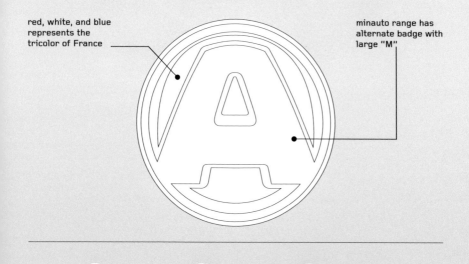

red, white, and blue represents the tricolor of France

minauto range has alternate badge with large "M"

000.000.000.030
#B3B3B3

000.100.100.000
#FF0000

100.070.000.060
#001F66

ALFA ROMEO

FOUNDED
June 24 1910 (Milan, Italy)

FOUNDER(S)
Nicola Romeo

YEARS OF OPERATION
1910–present

BEST-KNOWN MODELS
Alfa Spider, Alfasud, GTV, 8C

This classic Italian marque is named for a combination of its original acronym A.L.F.A. (Anonima Lombarda Fabbrica Automobili) with founder Nicola Romeo, who assumed control of the company in 1915, five years after its creation. The company has been owned by the Fiat Group since 1986, and its identity remains heavily reliant on its motorsport heritage.

The company badge is one of the most intriguing in the motoring world. It originally came from draughtsman Romano Cattaneo and designer Giuseppe Merosi in 1910. The left-hand side features a red cross on a white background, which is the ancient symbol of Milan, where the company was founded. The man-eating serpent on the right is a heraldic device from the coat of arms of the Visconti, the family who ruled Milan in the Middle Ages.

The badge has reduced in size and complexity over the last century. The latest version of the logo was unveiled in 2015, 100 years after Romeo took over the company. It was designed by the Milan-based Robilant & Associati agency, which is responsible for redesigning other Fiat Group brands, including Fiat (see pages 80–83) and Lancia (see pages 120–123). Alfa's more contemporary badge was reduced to three colors, switching the pale-blue-and-white background for a textured silver and introducing a fresh custom-designed serif typeface.

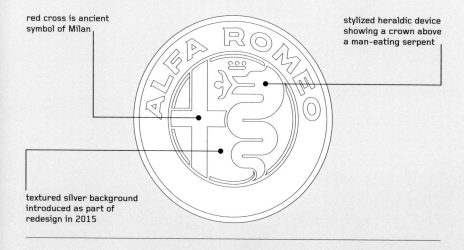

red cross is ancient symbol of Milan

stylized heraldic device showing a crown above a man-eating serpent

textured silver background introduced as part of redesign in 2015

000.000.000.030 #B3B3B3	000.100.100.010 #E60000	100.010.080.030 #00A124	100.080.020.030 #00248F

ARIEL

FOUNDED
1999 (Somerset, UK)

FOUNDER(S)
Simon Saunders

YEARS OF OPERATION
2001–present

BEST-KNOWN MODELS
Ariel Atom

The Ariel Atom is an extraordinary high-performance road car with no roof or windows but sensational performance. Its acceleration—0–60 mph (0–96 kph) in well under three seconds—has won awards and competitions. The Atom held the record for the fastest lap of the test track of British TV show *Top Gear* for two years. (The record was broken by the Pagani Huayra in 2013, and the McLaren 675LT in 2016.)

The Atom may be a futuristic supercar, but Ariel is one of the oldest manufacturers in the UK. Its first vehicle was a "penny farthing" bicycle in 1870. It continued to build motorcycles and specialist sports cars until ceasing production in the 1970s. The marque was revived by designer Simon Saunders in the late 1990s. He scribbled out the idea for the Ariel badge on the back of a book while taking a train to London. It clearly shows a futuristic capital letter "A," but the design can also be interpreted as a road disappearing into the distance. An alternative view is that the badge represents aerodynamics in action or shows a plan view of the Atom itself. In either case, it certainly bears no relation to the original Ariel company logo, which, although it has varied over the years, always featured the word "Ariel" in capital letters.

Today a small number of engineers build the Ariel vehicles by hand at a factory in rural Somerset, England. The various incarnations of the Atom have recently been joined by a motorcycle and extreme off-road buggy vehicle.

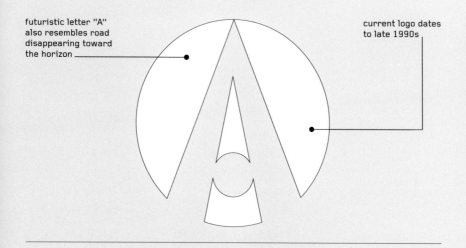

futuristic letter "A" also resembles road disappearing toward the horizon

current logo dates to late 1990s

000.090.080.000
#FF1933

ASTON MARTIN

FOUNDED
1913 (London, UK)

FOUNDER(S)
Martin and Robert Bamford

YEARS OF OPERATION
1913–present

BEST-KNOWN MODELS
DB5, Vantage, Vanquish

A single British carmaker has gradually cornered the market in producing thoroughbred sports cruisers that come with a throaty muscular engine and traditional leather-and-wood trimmed cabin. Over the last century Aston Martin has evolved from humble beginnings to become a world-famous independent marque.

It began as a joint project by two London car salesmen just before the First World War. Ten years of financial struggles followed, ending with a relaunch in 1927. That's when the old AM badge was scrapped and a distinctive winged emblem appeared, featuring the words "Aston Martin" in capitals over a pair of upswept wings. By 1932 the logo had been refined to almost its present form. Only a dedicated enthusiast could tell the 1932 badge from the current one. One of the differences is the number of feathers on each wing, which have varied over the years. Another is the removal of a hyphen from the name.

Befitting a marque that trumpets its traditional craftsmanship, every Aston Martin badge is handmade by Vaughtons in Birmingham's Jewellery Quarter, using computer-aided design templates, metalworking skills, and 21 stages of chroming, baking, and polishing.

The turning point in the history of the Aston Martin brand was, of course, the choice of the DB5 as the car for fictional special agent James Bond in the 1960s. Since then the company has been able to use that hint of glamour to survive as an independent manufacturer in an increasingly competitive marketplace.

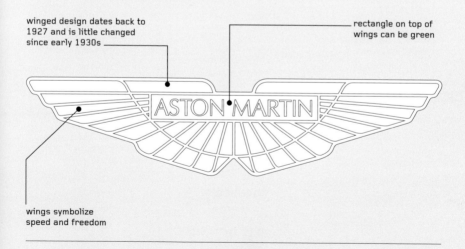

winged design dates back to 1927 and is little changed since early 1930s

rectangle on top of wings can be green

wings symbolize speed and freedom

000.000.000.030
#B3B3B3

060.070.050.070
#1F1726

AUDI

FOUNDED
1910 (Saxony, Germany)

FOUNDER(S)
August Horch

YEARS OF OPERATION
1910–present

BEST-KNOWN MODELS
Quattro, A4, TT, R8

One of today's most recognizable motoring badges is the four-ring symbol of the Audi brand. The emblem symbolizes the merger of four previously independent German manufacturers in 1932. Audi, DKW, Horch, and Wanderer joined forces to create the Auto Union marque. Initially the marques' original badges appeared inside each ring. These were later dropped and "Auto Union" imposed over the top in a rectangle.

Volkswagen (VW) took over Auto Union in the 1960s and merged it with another German motor manufacturer, NSU, in 1969. This didn't add another ring to the badge. VW did, however, reintroduce the Audi brand and it became the Group's upscale arm. Audi still forms part of the giant VW empire, which now also includes makers as diverse as Skoda (see 188–189), Seat (see pages 186–187), Bentley (see pages 28–29), Lamborghini (see pages 118–119), and Bugatti (see pages 36–39). Audi is now one of the biggest-selling luxury car brands in the world.

The World Olympic Committee took Audi to the International Trademark Court in 1995, claiming the badge was too similar to its five-ring emblem, which was designed in 1912. The court found that the designs were sufficiently different, however, and the carmaker's badge was allowed to stand. The rings have been updated with each generation of design trends, but these have been limited to subtle changes in shading and the accompanying typeface.

four rings symbolize 1932
merger of Audi, DKW, Horch,
and Wanderer

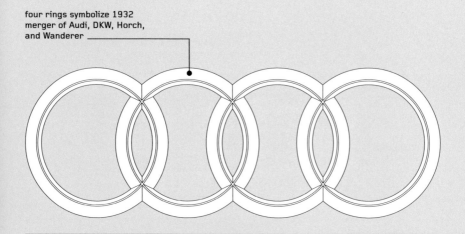

000.000.000.030
#B3B3B3

BENTLEY

FOUNDED
1919 (London, UK)

FOUNDER(S)
W.O. and H. M. Bentley

YEARS OF OPERATION
1919–present

BEST-KNOWN MODELS
Bentley "Blower," Continental, Bentayga, Mulsanne

The symbolic use of wings was a familiar device for early motoring emblem makers. However, Bentley had more excuse for their use than most—the company started out by making engines for Sopwith Camel biplanes during the First World War.

Soon the company became associated with high-performance cars and later, more luxurious grand tourers. Eventually, in 1998, Bentley was taken over by the Volkswagen Group, but it still produces its vehicles in a factory in Crewe, Cheshire in northwest England.

Despite the changes in ownership over the last 100 years, the marque's badge has remained pretty consistent. It is still a simple white capital "B" on a roundel with a pair of silver bird's wings either side. The badge is a timeless classic that still looks as relevant on today's 190 mph (305 kmph) Mulsanne Speed as it did on the pre-war supercharged "Bentley Blower."

A more detailed examination reveals the slight changes to the badges over the last century. For example, the emblems of pre-war "Derby" cars featured ten feathers on one side, 11 on the other. Earlier cars, however, had 13 and 14 on each side. There was a period after the Second World War when ten feathers featured symmetrically on each side, but modern cars have reverted to ten feathers on one side, 11 on the other. The company has more recently introduced varied colors for the badge roundel. These can be red, green, or black, depending on the precise model.

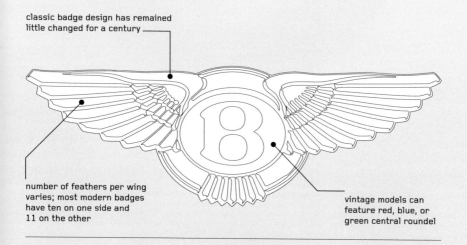

classic badge design has remained little changed for a century

number of feathers per wing varies; most modern badges have ten on one side and 11 on the other

vintage models can feature red, blue, or green central roundel

000.000.000.030
#B3B3B3

000.000.000.100
#000000

BMW

FOUNDED
March 7 1916 (Munich, Germany)

FOUNDER(S)
Franz Josef Popp

YEARS OF OPERATION
1917–present

BEST-KNOWN MODELS
three-series, five-series, i8

In July 1917, during the First World War, Franz Josef Popp registered the name of his new aircraft engine manufacturing company, Bayerische Motoren Werke. This fledgling engineering works had emerged from another aircraft engine manufacturer. A few months later, Popp registered a trademark for his new BMW operation. It featured a black ring with the letters "BMW" at the top. Inside the ring were light-blue and white quadrants, signifying the colors of the Bavarian flag where the company was based.

The new company didn't start building motorcycles until 1923, and then expanded into cars around 1928. It was just after this that customers first started interpreting the BMW company badge as a rotating propeller; until then it had just been four colored quadrants. This followed a company advertisement for its aircraft engines featuring the badge superimposed over a spinning propeller.

Originally the badge lettering was gold, but this was standardized as silver in the 1950s. By the 1960s, the typeface had been changed to the present neat sans-serif font. A temporary variation appeared during the 1970s and 1980s, when the main roundel was surrounded by the colors of BMW's motorsport division: blue, purple, and red. Most recently, in 1997, the badge was given a slightly three-dimensional appearance with subtle shading to make the printed form stand out. Despite these minor changes, the design has remained remarkably consistent, and this simple but enduring badge is consistently ranked among the top-ten commercial symbols of all time.

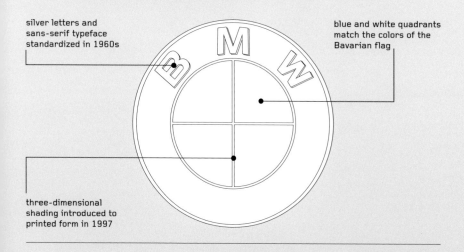

silver letters and sans-serif typeface standardized in 1960s

blue and white quadrants match the colors of the Bavarian flag

three-dimensional shading introduced to printed form in 1997

000.000.000.000
#FFFFFF

 000.000.000.030
#B3B3B3

090.050.020.000
#1980CC

 000.000.000.100
#000000

BORGWARD

FOUNDED
1921 (Bremen, Germany)

FOUNDER(S)
Carl Borgward

YEARS OF OPERATION
1924–1961 and 2008–present

BEST-KNOWN MODELS
Isabella, BX7

Maverick entrepreneur Carl Borgward's motor manufacturing empire embraced three brands: Lloyd (small cars), Goliath (mid-range cars and trucks), and his namesake company, which produced luxury cars and big trucks. These Bremen-based factories boomed after the First World War and sold more than 100,000 vehicles in 1959 alone. In the late 1950s Borgward's 1.5-liter Isabella became Germany's top motoring export.

Despite introducing advanced engineering, such as air suspension and automatic transmission, Borgward suffered financial problems and it is said that the determinedly individual operator was squeezed out of the market by his German rivals. Borgward ceased production in 1961, but in 2008 Carl's grandson Christian was able to relaunch the brand with Chinese investment. Its new BX7 SUV is built and sold in China, though there are plans to assemble versions back in Bremen.

The classic Borgward badge is a relatively simple diamond divided into red-and-white quarters, with "Borgward" in capitals across the center. The red and white match the colors on the coat of arms of the company's home city of Bremen. Sometimes the badge was mounted between two wings; other times it formed an unusually modern display in the center of the radiator grille. Today's revived Borgward badge has been slightly modernized with a more contemporary typeface and more prominent silver diamond surround, but the link to the original brand is still instantly recognizable.

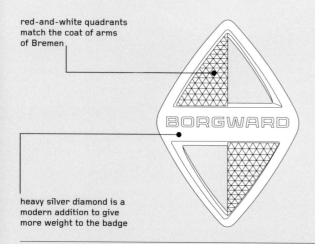

red-and-white quadrants match the coat of arms of Bremen

heavy silver diamond is a modern addition to give more weight to the badge

 000.000.000.030
#B3B3B3

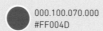 000.100.070.000
#FF004D

 000.000.000.100
#000000

BRISTOL CARS

FOUNDED
1945 (Bristol, UK)

FOUNDER(S)
George White and Reginald Verdon-Smith

YEARS OF OPERATION
1947–2011

BEST-KNOWN MODELS
411, Blenheim, Fighter

Bristol Cars was created at the end of the Second World War from redundant airplane factories combined with what remained of the ailing Frazer Nash sports car company. It was based alongside an aerodrome in Bristol, England.

The company was always outside the mainstream of the motoring industry. It made hand-built luxury sports cars but often refused to reveal how many cars it made or sold. It also avoided advertising completely, claiming that word of mouth was enough for its customers.

The company struggled through several difficult periods until it finally stopped production because of financial problems in 2011.

Shortly after, the Bristol marque was taken over by Kamkorp Autokraft Group. Various plans and prototypes have been announced since, but as yet no new production cars have appeared.

The Bristol badge has always been a black roundel with a silver rim. In the center is a silver shield on a red background containing a simplified version of the official shield of the nautical city of Bristol, which features images of a ship, a cliff, and a castle. This badge appeared on the grille, hood, and sometimes wheel hubs of Bristol cars.

The new Kamkorp-owned Bristol Cars company still uses the original 60-year-old logo as its own.

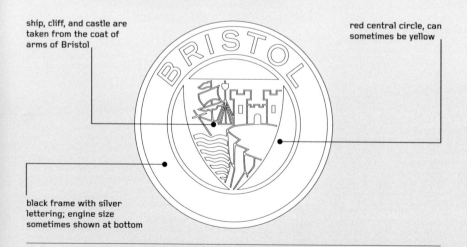

ship, cliff, and castle are taken from the coat of arms of Bristol

red central circle, can sometimes be yellow

black frame with silver lettering; engine size sometimes shown at bottom

 000.000.000.030 #B3B3B3

 000.080.075.000 #CB5040

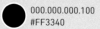 000.000.000.100 #FF3340

BUGATTI

FOUNDED
1909 (Alsace, France)

FOUNDER(S)
Ettore Bugatti

YEARS OF OPERATION
1909–1952 and 1987–present

BEST-KNOWN MODELS
Type 41 Royale, Type 57 Atlantic, EB110, Veyron

Ettore Bugatti considered himself an artist when he founded a car company in Alsace in 1909. Many of the cars he produced between the wars have been hailed as among the most beautiful ever made. Today, the rare Royale and Atlantic models still command record prices when they appear at auction.

After Ettore died in 1947, the brand slowly disappeared from the scene. It changed hands but no new Bugattis were built until the rare, Italian-built EB110 supercar in the 1990s, a model once owned by Michael Schumacher.

Volkswagen bought the marque in 1998 and in 2005 introduced to the market the Veyron, an extraordinary high-performance, high-priced supercar. Overnight it transformed the image of the brand.

The Bugatti badge, however, has remained remarkably constant for more than a century. The distinctive symbol of a reversed "E" and "B" fused together was designed by Ettore's father, a noted jewelry designer. Ettore even used the logo on his personal set of cutlery.

On the car badge this logo stands in a red oval above "Bugatti" in white capitals with black drop shadow. The oval is surrounded by a silver rim containing 60 red dots. The origin of the dots has long been a mystery. Some say they represent small pearls, others that they link back to the red safety wires originally threaded through early Bugatti engines. Alternatively, they may be simply a decorative device employed by someone whose specialism was making jewelry.

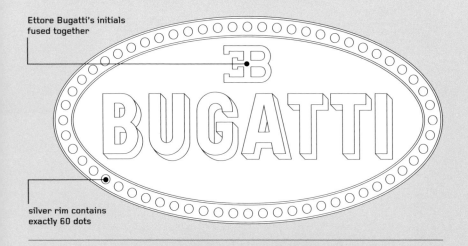

Ettore Bugatti's initials fused together

silver rim contains exactly 60 dots

000.000.000.000
#FFFFFF

010.100.090.000
#E60019

000.000.000.100
#000000

Profile: ETTORE BUGATTI

NATIONALITY
French (naturalized)

BORN
September 15 1881 (Milan, Italy)

DIED
August 21 1947 (Paris, France)

FOUNDER
Automobiles E. Bugatti

Ettore Arco Isidoro Bugatti was born in Milan, Italy, in September 1881. The young Bugatti was surrounded by artistic influences; his father Carlo was an important art nouveau furniture and jewelry designer, and his paternal grandfather Giovanni was an architect and sculptor.

He received very little formal training as an engineer but displayed a natural talent around engines, which was recognized when he took up his first apprenticeship with bicycle manufacturer Prinetti & Stucchi at the age of 17. During this period Bugatti built a motorized tricycle, and shortly afterward built his first car. Named the Bugatti Type 1 and produced by Prinetti & Stucchi in 1898, it utilized two separate pairs of engines mounted on either side of the rear axle.

Bugatti went on to develop a second prototype, which won a prize at the Milan Trade Fair in 1901. As a result, the manufacturer Baron de Dietrich offered Bugatti a job and the relationship lasted until 1905 when Bugatti and businessman Émile Mathis formed a company that allowed Bugatti to begin making his own cars. After parting company with Mathis in 1906, Bugatti joined the Cologne-based engine manufacturer Deutz as Production Director, while continuing to produce prototype cars including the Type 8/9 and Type 10 at home in his basement.

Bugatti departed from Deutz in 1909 and the first true Bugatti, the T13, began production from his newly established factory based in an ex-dyeworks plant in Molsheim, Alsace. Alongside the T13 and to help support his own company financially, Bugatti continued to design cars under license for other manufacturers, including Peugeot.

The outbreak of the First World War enforced a break in production and Bugatti moved his family to Milan and then Paris, where he produced several designs for aircraft engines. After the war he returned to Molsheim (now French rather than German territory) to build the lightweight sports cars he is best known for, achieving considerable success on the racing circuit. By this time his son Jean was also involved with the company and in 1934 the Type 57, arguably Bugatti's crowning glory as a designer, had entered production.

Sadly, Jean Bugatti was killed while test driving a Type 57 C in August 1939 and Ettore's wife Barbara died shortly afterward. The factory in Molsheim was destroyed during the Second World War and Bugatti lost control of the property and therefore the company, which eventually filed for bankruptcy in 1952. Ettore died in Paris on August 21 1947, but his legacy lives on in the Molsheim factory, rebuilt by Volkswagen, who have owned the Bugatti brand since 1998.

BUICK

FOUNDED
1899 (Michigan, USA)

FOUNDER(S)
David Dunbar Buick

YEARS OF OPERATION
1899–present

BEST-KNOWN MODELS
Roadmaster, Skylark, Riviera, LeSabre

America's oldest surviving motoring brand has today been relegated to a strategic part of the General Motors (GM) empire. The Buick badge is used on GM's premium vehicles to lift them above mainstream level—but without intruding into the lofty region occupied by Cadillac (see pages 44–45).

Scottish-American David Buick's Michigan-based company made its first vehicle at the end of the 19th century. It soon became the biggest producer in the USA and pioneered the first overhead-valve engines. The successful company bought up smaller rivals and called its new conglomeration General Motors.

Buicks of the 1930s featured a dashing silver figure as a radiator mascot, but the most enduring symbol of the marque is the "tri-shield." This is an arrangement of three shields in a diagonal formation. The shields themselves are each split by a diagonal silver band. The logo is derived from David Buick's Scottish family coat of arms, which was a red shield split by a diagonal line with a stag above and a cross below. A single shield with this motif was introduced in the 1930s. Previously Buicks had simply worn the word "Buick" as their emblem.

The single shield became three in 1959, to represent the marque's three models: LeSabre, Invicta, and Electra. Originally the trio were colored a patriotic red, white, and blue, but today the badge is simply a chrome outline of the three within a circle. Surveys conducted in the USA have found that Buick's tri-shield is one of the most recognizable and trusted auto badges.

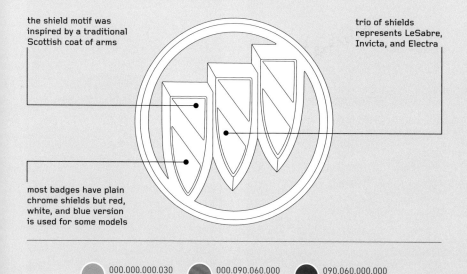

the shield motif was inspired by a traditional Scottish coat of arms

trio of shields represents LeSabre, Invicta, and Electra

most badges have plain chrome shields but red, white, and blue version is used for some models

000.000.000.030
#B3B3B3

000.090.060.000
#FF1966

090.060.000.000
#1966FF

BUICK: Evolution

The emblem of the longest surviving motoring marque in the USA has been through some drastic changes. In the last 100 years Buick's badge has evolved from a simple name script to today's graphic triple shield.

1903

1903

1913

1913

1930

1937

1939

1949

1949

1949

1959

1990

CADILLAC

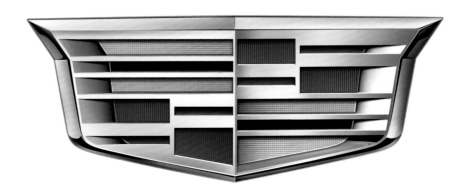

FOUNDED
August 1902 (Detroit, USA)

FOUNDER(S)
William Murphy, Lemuel Bowen, and Henry M. Leland

YEARS OF OPERATION
1902–present

BEST-KNOWN MODELS
Fleetwood, Eldorado, DeVille, Escalade

Cadillac is the foremost luxury brand of the giant U.S. General Motors (GM) empire. It is world famous for its large, well-appointed, refined, powerful, and comfortable limousines that date back over a century.

However, the Cadillac company actually started as an independent carmaker and was already established by the time GM took it over in 1909. Cadillac had been founded by financiers in Detroit in 1902. They named it for Antoine de la Mothe Cadillac, a colorful and controversial 17th-century French explorer who had founded the marque's home city.

The new company badge was closely based on Monsieur Cadillac's purportedly noble French coat of arms. Since then,

however, historians have cast doubt on the Frenchman's aristocratic pedigree and many now believe he was a fraud, that he invented the distinguished name, and stole a neighbor's heraldic symbols.

Nevertheless, Cadillac cars have continued to carry a version of this coat of arms. The original, rather complex heraldic device, featuring a crown, birds, stripes, and a wreath, has gradually been simplified as design fashions changed over the decades. Eventually the badge has been pared down to today's graphic shield emblem. The current logo appears so divorced from Cadillac's original coat of arms that many believe it is more inspired by Dutch abstract artist Piet Mondrian, who painted similar colored geometric designs.

today's badge is a graphic simplification of what was once a complex coat of arms

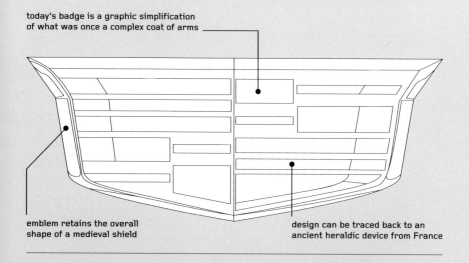

emblem retains the overall shape of a medieval shield

design can be traced back to an ancient heraldic device from France

 000.000.000.030
#B3B3B3

 000.010.060.000
#FFE666

 000.100.100.010
#E60000

 100.100.000.010
#0000E6

CADILLAC: Evolution

The Cadillac marque has been redesigned around the central theme of French explorer Antoine de la Mothe Cadillac's coat of arms no less than 38 times. Here are 12 of the key stages of that evolution.

1906

1909

1934

1941

1942

1947

1947

1949

1952

1970

1972

1972

CATERHAM

FOUNDED
1959 (Caterham, UK)

FOUNDER(S)
Graham Nearn

YEARS OF OPERATION
1973–present

BEST-KNOWN MODEL
Seven

The back-to-basics Lotus Seven sports car had been a cult success among British driving aficionados in the 1960s. In the 1970s, however, Lotus announced it was discontinuing the model.

Caterham, one of Lotus's biggest dealers, bought the rights to keep making the little roadster in 1973, and so the company transformed from retailer to producer.

The small manufacturer has continued to stick to small-volume, specialist lightweight sports machines with rear-wheel drive and two cramped seats, including the Seven. The cars are constructed from simple aluminum sheets fixed to a sturdy tubular steel chassis.

Caterham offers few concessions to comfort or luxury, and the main difference between the models has been the engines from other manufacturers and their extreme performance and handling ability, which is mostly down to the very low weight of the cars.

The badging of Caterham's cars might appear makeshift, but the cars are unique, so branding is not necessarily the same consideration that it would be for a multinational corporation. Most cars still use a version of the original Lotus 7 badge: a figure "7" within a shield on the front grille. Sometimes this is placed in a roundel and used as a small badge elsewhere on the car. On some occasions it includes a laurel wreath. The word "Caterham" has also been presented in different ways. The most recent corporate logo features half a British flag in green with the word "Caterham" in italic capitals in the center.

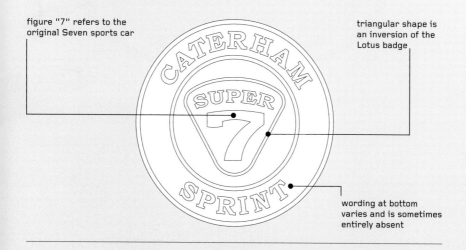

figure "7" refers to the original Seven sports car

triangular shape is an inversion of the Lotus badge

wording at bottom varies and is sometimes entirely absent

000.000.000.000
#FFFFFF

000.030.095.000
#FFB30D

100.040.100.050
#004D00

CHANGAN

FOUNDED
1862 (Chongqing, China)

FOUNDER(S)
State government

YEARS OF OPERATION
1957–present

BEST-KNOWN MODELS
Yuexiang, Eado, Benni

The state-owned Changan Automobile Company is one of the "big four" Chinese carmakers. The company claims to have an industrial history dating back 155 years, but most industry observers accept that it actually evolved from a smaller company called Changan Factory in the 1960s. The factory had started assembling military-style jeeps from 1957 and sold them under the name Yangtze River.

Changan grew quickly from these humble beginnings, however. At first, it became primarily a minivan maker but soon began producing its own cars, too. The small four-door Benni hatchback appeared in 2009 and was driven all the way up to Everest Base Camp as a promotional stunt.

The original logo—a red arch within an oval—was replaced by a new, more impressive Changan badge in 2010. The new sculpted V-shaped emblem on a blue plaque was fitted to all Changan's cars, while the old badge remained on the commercial vehicles. The company name was redesigned, too, with the contemporary capitals giving a hint of Asian modernity.

Today, the company runs joint car-making operations with Ford, Mazda, Peugeot Citroën, and Suzuki to build their cars for the Chinese market. Changan also builds its own range of cars, SUVs, and vans. Exports are growing and it has established an assembly plant in Russia. Expect to spot the Changan badge on vehicles around the world within a few years.

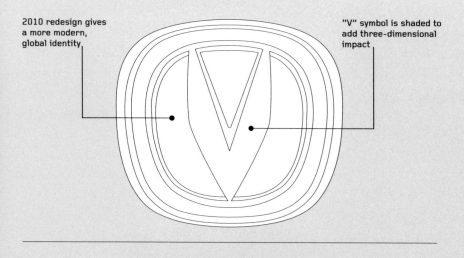

2010 redesign gives a more modern, global identity

"V" symbol is shaded to add three-dimensional impact

100.080.040.025
#002673

000.000.000.100
#000000

CHEVROLET

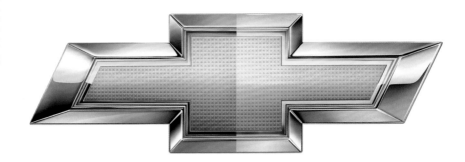

FOUNDED
November 3 1911 (Detroit, USA)

FOUNDER(S)
Louis Chevrolet and William C. Durant

YEARS OF OPERATION
1911–present

BEST-KNOWN MODELS
Corvette, Camaro, Impala, Bel Air, Chevelle, Volt, C/K

Swiss racing driver Louis Chevrolet helped entrepreneur William C. Durant launch a car company in Detroit, Michigan. The first model, the rather grand Classic Six, appeared with a slightly messy italic script logo. But soon there was a distinctive emblem: the classic Chevrolet "bow tie." This first appeared in 1914 on the new H Series and L Series models and, with only small adaptations, still appears on Chevrolet vehicles today.

There are two competing theories about where this idea came from. Official Chevy history says Durant saw it on French hotel wallpaper and tore off a section to remind him when he returned to America. However, other automotive historians claim he simply copied the logo belonging to "Coalettes" coal ("the little coals with the big heat"), which he came across in a Virginia newspaper. Whichever is correct, Chevrolet has grown to become a major global brand. It is such an integral part of the success of the General Motors (GM) group that the word "Chevy" is often used as a synonym for GM.

The original badge was blue with "Chevrolet" in capitals across the center. Over the decades, Chevrolet used different colors to distinguish its sports cars from ordinary cars and trucks, but eventually returned to one simple logo. The gold bow-tie badge is now a bold, gold cross with a chunky chrome surround.

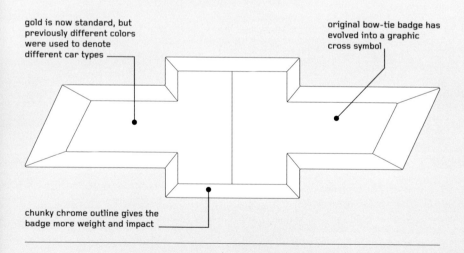

gold is now standard, but previously different colors were used to denote different car types

original bow-tie badge has evolved into a graphic cross symbol

chunky chrome outline gives the badge more weight and impact

000.000.000.030
#B3B3B3

010.025.080.000
#E6BF33

CHRYSLER

FOUNDED
June 6 1925 (Detroit, USA)

FOUNDER(S)
Walter Chrysler

YEARS OF OPERATION
1925–present

BEST-KNOWN MODELS
Imperial, Jeep Cherokee, Dodge Jeep Ram, Dodge Viper, Chrysler 300

This marque was named for its founder, former railroad mechanic turned motor-factory production manager, Walter Chrysler. He made a fortune running other car companies before finally setting up his own in 1925. Chrysler was wealthy enough to build the towering landmark Chrysler Building in New York and oversaw the creation of his own premium motoring brand. The company is still a major global brand, although now it forms part of Fiat Chrysler Automobiles (FCA).

Early Chryslers came with a complex badge designed by Oliver Clark, a member of Chrysler's engineering team. It mimicked a traditional wax seal with ribbons, and had the name "Chrysler" across the center. A tiny lightning bolt suggested power, while a rope border symbolized strength. This was all set within a pair of chrome wings and a frame, topped by a crown and the Chrysler script. More than any other American carmaker, however, Chrysler's emblems changed with the tide of fashion. Some 1960s cars had a big letter "C" as the badge; others had a row of crowns. A golden lion was chosen for a short while, then an eagle.

From the 1970s to the 1990s, Chrysler used the "pentastar" emblem, a five-pointed star within a pentagon. It had been chosen from a selection of 800 different designs produced by a team of designers because it was a classic but memorable geometric shape. The pentastar was dropped after the Fiat merger, however. Today's Chrysler badge is an elegant wide chrome wing containing the brand name in capitals on a blue background.

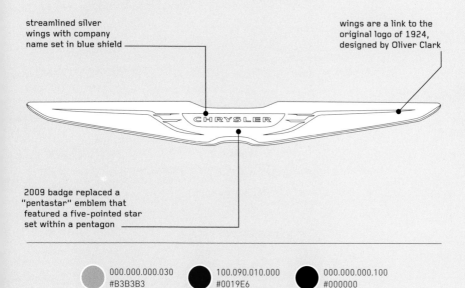

streamlined silver
wings with company
name set in blue shield

wings are a link to the
original logo of 1924,
designed by Oliver Clark

2009 badge replaced a
"pentastar" emblem that
featured a five-pointed star
set within a pentagon

000.000.000.030
#B3B3B3

100.090.010.000
#0019E6

000.000.000.100
#000000

CITROËN

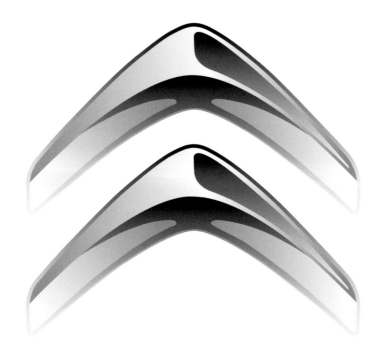

FOUNDED
1919 (Paris, France)

FOUNDER(S)
André Citroën

YEARS OF OPERATION
1919–present

BEST-KNOWN MODELS
Traction Avant, 2CV, DS, BX, Picasso

Over the last century, the car company founded by enterprising industrialist André Citroën has developed a reputation for creating groundbreaking vehicles. Citroën landmarks have included the first European front-wheel-drive car (Traction Avant, 1934) and the first disc brakes in Europe (DS, 1955). The 2CV of 1948 was a pioneering small, light, cheap car for the mass market and the BX of 1982 was a front runner in the use of plastic body parts.

The double chevron that adorns the front of Citroën cars dates back to the first days of the company. In 1900, 22-year-old André visited Poland and noticed that local cotton mills used distinctive chevron-shaped gears. The young engineer realized

this could have potential elsewhere when made from steel. He developed this idea into the double-helical gear system, which revolutionized transmissions.

The chevron gears were so important to Citroën that he made them the company badge. With only small variations, the chevrons have graced the front of Citroëns ever since, often being prominently built into the hood or grille. This has made them one of the best-known motoring emblems.

When Citroën wanted to establish a premium sub-brand with its DS range in 2009, however, it dropped the chevrons and used a different DS logo. The chevrons continue, meanwhile, on Citroën's more mainstream models.

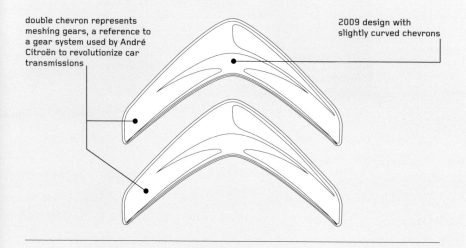

double chevron represents meshing gears, a reference to a gear system used by André Citroën to revolutionize car transmissions

2009 design with slightly curved chevrons

Profile: ANDRÉ CITROËN

NATIONALITY
French

BORN
February 5 1878 (Paris, France)

DIED
July 3 1935 (Paris, France)

FOUNDER
Citroën

Although André Citroën is remembered primarily for the automobile company he founded, his engineering credentials extend back to a time before he ever considered manufacturing a car. Citroën's Jewish father, Levie, was a Dutch diamond merchant while his mother, Masza, was Polish. His father committed suicide following a failed business venture when Citroën was only six years old and his mother died during his teenage years, but Citroën nonetheless managed to overcome these losses and graduated from the prestigious École Polytechnique in 1900, albeit with disappointing grades.

With limited job prospects, Citroën joined the army as an engineering officer, where he gained a wealth of practical experience. While visiting family in Poland during a period of leave, he observed carpenters making wooden gears featuring a herringbone pattern for use in cotton mills. Realizing the engineering opportunities afforded by gears of this type manufactured from steel, Citroën obtained a patent and in 1904, along with several business associates, he opened a small production facility to manufacture double-helical gearwheels. The company, Hinstin, Frères, Citroën et Cie, quickly prospered and the invention credited to Citroën brought him wealth and widespread recognition. It is these chevron-shaped gears that provide the Citroën logo with its distinctive shape.

When the First World War broke out, Citroën was still a captain in the army reserves and returned to active service in the artillery. A large-scale shortage of ammunition prompted him to suggest to his superiors that he apply his considerable knowledge of mass-production techniques to the problem, and Citroën was given the responsibility of supplying all French munitions plants with raw materials and manufacturing guidance. During wartime the workforce was largely female, and Citroën is credited as one of the earliest pioneers of workers' rights and benefits. He introduced maternity leave for his female workers, provided medical and dental facilities for all employees, built a workers' gymnasium at his factory, and even provided a day care center.

Following the war and involvement in various projects, including the aborted development of a steam car, Citroën founded the Citroën Automobile company in 1919. Keen to repurpose his manufacturing plant back to civilian use, and after observing what Henry Ford was achieving in the United States, car manufacturing seemed the obvious venture to pursue. His collaboration with the American engineer Edward G. Budd produced the first all-steel car body in 1925, and by the early 1930s Citroën had become the fourth-largest automobile manufacturer in the world.

Unfortunately rising production costs resulted in bankruptcy for the company in 1934 and it was taken over by its main creditor, the tire manufacturer Michelin. Citroën died from stomach cancer on July 3 1935 and is buried in Paris's famous Cimetière du Montparnasse.

CORVETTE

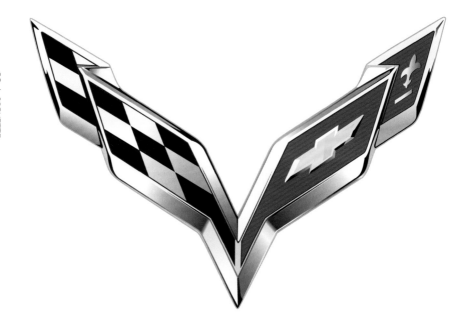

FOUNDED
June 30 1953 (Detroit, USA)

FOUNDER(S)
Louis Chevrolet

YEARS OF OPERATION
1953–present

BEST-KNOWN MODELS
Stingray, ZR1

Though not strictly a marque in its own right, the Corvette is one of the sporting jewels of Chevrolet's crown. The model has been a desirable part of American auto culture since the first version appeared in 1953. At the time of writing, there have been seven different generations of Corvette, including both coupés and convertibles. They've all been two-seaters and the designs have combined fiberglass or composite bodies with big engines to produce exhilarating performance.

How has this brand within a brand, that is itself part of the General Motors (GM) empire, been badged? When the original model was launched, Chevy bosses realized only at the last minute that a planned use of the nation's Stars and Stripes within the car logo was illegal at the time. So the first Corvette appeared with a twin-flag logo: a sporty checkered flag crossed with a red flag depicting the Chevrolet "bow-tie" (see page 52) and a heraldic fleur-de-lis symbol recalling the French origins of company founder Louis Chevrolet.

The badge has varied with different versions of the Corvette. Some featured a circle of flags around the words "Chevrolet Corvette." By the 1980s, the flags had become angular. The fleur-de-lis disappeared, leaving the prominent Chevrolet bow tie. Then, for the millennium, the old French symbol returned.

In the latest Corvette badges, the flags are still there but have become almost graphic symbols, like two wings rimmed with chrome.

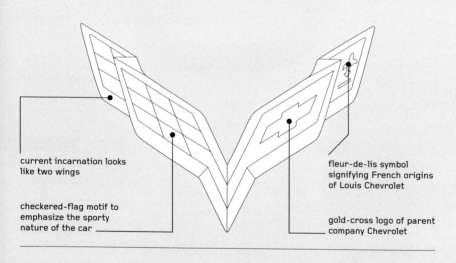

current incarnation looks like two wings

checkered-flag motif to emphasize the sporty nature of the car

fleur-de-lis symbol signifying French origins of Louis Chevrolet

gold-cross logo of parent company Chevrolet

000.000.000.030
#B3B3B3

010.025.080.000
#E6BF33

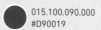
015.100.090.000
#D90019

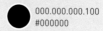
000.000.000.100
#000000

DACIA

FOUNDED
1966 (Mioveni, Romania)

FOUNDER(S)
State-owned

YEARS OF OPERATION
1966–present

BEST-KNOWN MODELS
Duster, Sandero, Logan

In just a decade, Dacia has gone from a little-known Romanian marque to a global automotive power. Under the stewardship of the Renault Group, the low-cost brand has become a bestseller in some markets, and highly rated in most others. Its factory is now Europe's fifth biggest car plant.

The company was founded in 1966 under the name Uzina de Autoturisme Pitesti (UAP). Dacia, the name that has appeared on all the cars, refers to the old name for the region now known as Romania, where it is based. Dacia originally made rebadged or slightly modified versions of old Renault vehicles. In 1999, Renault took over the company and transformed production so that, by 2004, a new wave of globally competitive cars emerged. These new value-for-money Dacias were well received.

This fast-moving history has been accompanied by some similarly rapid changes to the logo. The present Dacia emblem is a plain chrome device with the word "Dacia" in blue capitals. It resembles a shield, a buckle, or perhaps a car door handle. Its simplicity conveys the brand image of no-frills, cost-effective products.

Early Dacia badges were shield-shaped and featured a traditional Romanian symbol of a stylized eagle with spread wings, perched on top of a mountain. Later, the eagle was dropped and the word "Dacia" appeared in an elaborate typeface evocative of Eastern Europe. The typeface was later simplified within a simple blue shield, and then the current design took over in 2008.

shape echoes the original shield-shaped badge

plain typeface complements the brand's no-frills image

simple design emphasizes the rugged, unpretentious image of the company

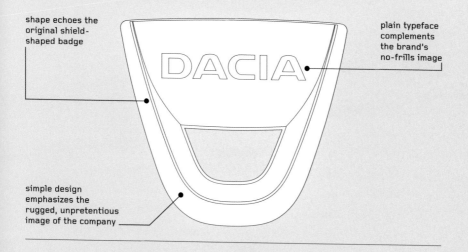

000.000.000.030
#B3B3B3

090.060.000.050
#0D3380

DAEWOO

FOUNDED
1982 (South Korea)

FOUNDER(S)
Kim Woo Choong

YEARS OF OPERATION
1982–2002

BEST-KNOWN MODELS
Matiz, Lanos, Nubira, Leganza, Espero

The rapid rise and even faster fall of Daewoo demonstrates the harsh reality of today's global motoring market. Daewoo's brief moment in the sun started—and ended—in the inglorious world of "badge engineering."

The giant Korean Daewoo Group took over Shinjin Motors, which had been making and rebranding clones of foreign cars for decades. But Daewoo had big plans for its home-based marque. Daewoo Motors was established in 1982 and a wave of new models followed, with extensive global promotion. The cars improved. Exports soared. Within 20 years, however, an Asian financial crash led to a takeover by America's General Motors (GM). Gradually, all of Daewoo's models were rebadged as Chevrolets.

The Daewoo slogans went from "A different kind of car company? That'll be the Daewoo" to "Daewoo has grown up enough to become Chevrolet." A few years later, Daewoo had disappeared as a motoring name.

Through all those years of upheaval, the Daewoo badge was repeatedly changed. At first, it featured simply neat, capitalized letters spelling "Daewoo." Variations in international markets included a stylized chrome crown and a graphic resembling a fountain.

As financial troubles continued, however, the Daewoo marque was considered a sales hindrance. Its new parent company, GM, couldn't wait to replace the discredited logos with its own Chevy badges.

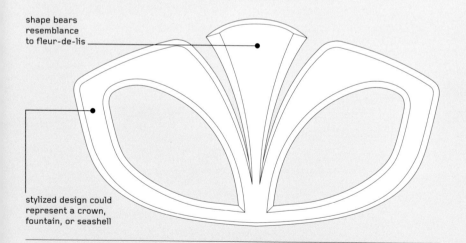

shape bears resemblance to fleur-de-lis

stylized design could represent a crown, fountain, or seashell

000.000.000.030
#B3B3B3

DAF

FOUNDED
1928 (Eindhoven, Netherlands)

FOUNDER(S)
Hub and Wim van Doorne

YEARS OF OPERATION
1958–1975 (car division)

BEST-KNOWN MODELS
Variomatic, DAF 66

Van Doorne's Aanhangwagen Fabriek (Van Doorne's Trailer Factory) had been a prewar engineering workshop in the Netherlands. Brothers Hub and Wim van Doorne had helped to grow the company from a small blacksmith's shop into a versatile industrial business.

Eventually, their operation abbreviated its name to DAF and began making trucks. After the war, DAF added car-making to its roster, too. The company's best-known models used a pioneering belt-drive system that was considered ahead of its time. Other manufacturers noticed. Volvo took a great interest, eventually buying a controlling share of DAF cars and badging its designs as Volvos. After that, DAF's car arm lost its separate identity in a series of takeovers, but its truck-making division is still going strong, albeit under the ownership of the American Paccar Inc.

When the trailer factory became the vehicle factory, there was, of course, a new logo: the new name "DAF" above the graphic of a leaf-spring suspension system and a wheel containing the words "Eindhoven, Nederland" to show where the company was based.

The badge suited the front of trucks but perhaps not the new range of DAF cars. So, the cars were given a simple corporate emblem, the capital letters "DAF" in a plain sans-serif script in the center of the grille. The enduring truck division, meanwhile, has benefited from a chunky version of the three letters.

initials originate from "Van Doorne's Aanhangwagen Fabriek"

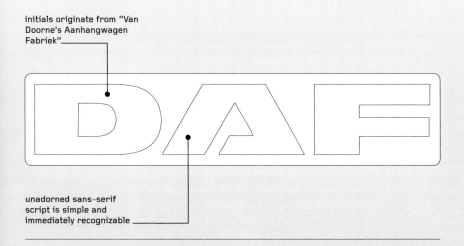

unadorned sans-serif script is simple and immediately recognizable

000.000.000.030
#B3B3B3

000.000.000.000
#FFFFFF

DAIHATSU

FOUNDED
1907 (Ikeda, Osaka Prefecture, Japan)

FOUNDER(S)
Professor Yoshiaki Yasunaga and Seishiro Tsurumi

YEARS OF OPERATION
1931–present

BEST-KNOWN MODELS
Charade, Fourtrak, Sirion, Terios

Founded in Osaka in 1907, Daihatsu is one of Japan's oldest car companies. Originally it was an engineering works focusing on trains and trucks called Hatsudoki. The company was renamed Daihatsu in 1951, a name derived from a rough combination of traditional Japanese characters for "Osaka engine manufacture." Even then, it took 12 years for the first proper new car to appear. Later, however, there followed a stream of innovative cars, SUVs, and vans.

Daihatsu became renowned for its miniature vehicles, called "kei cars," which initially were built to conform to Japanese size restrictions but became a cult success all over the world. Time wasn't kind to this distinctive carmaker. The Toyota Group completely took over Daihatsu in 2016. The brand has been withdrawn from many of the most competitive export markets, although it still makes and sells small cars in emerging markets, such as Indonesia.

The marque's logo evolved gradually along with the sophistication of the Japanese auto industry. At first it was a homely italic script on a gray oval, but in 1957 that was changed for italic capitals on a red pair of angular wings.

By the late 1970s the slicker-looking Daihatsu emblem was a very stylized capital "D." This appeared either on a red square with the word "Daihatsu" in capitals underneath or in chrome surrounded by a chrome circle.

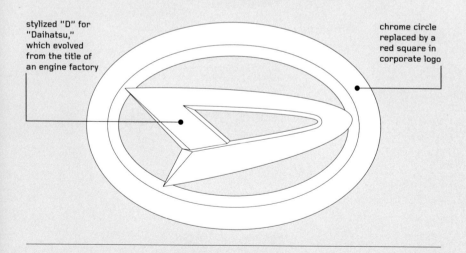

stylized "D" for "Daihatsu," which evolved from the title of an engine factory

chrome circle replaced by a red square in corporate logo

000.000.000.030
#B3B3B3

DATSUN

FOUNDED

1911 (Yokohama, Japan)

FOUNDER(S)

Masujiro Hashimoto

YEARS OF OPERATION

1914–1986 and 2013–present

BEST-KNOWN MODELS

Fairlady, Sunny, 280ZX Coupe, Go

Datsun is the marque that simply would not go away. Parent company Nissan tried to dump its old brand name in the 1980s. In the end, it took 10 years and around US$500m to change the company's badging, naming, signage, and publicity worldwide.

The Datsun name derived from a trio of car pioneers whose initials spelled "DAT," which appropriately means "dash like a startled rabbit" in Japanese. Later DAT became "son of DAT" (Datson) to market smaller cars. Then someone in marketing thought the rising "sun" was a more suitable Japanese image than "son," so the company name was changed to Datsun in 1934. The logo was the company name in capitals on a blue bar against a red sun.

Great export success followed but, behind the scenes, Nissan considered Datsun a minor "pet name" and wanted to use its own name instead.

Nissan eventually did emerge successfully from Datsun's shadow, but cars and memories don't disappear that easily. In a surprise U-turn in 2013, Nissan revived the Datsun brand as a badge for budget cars in emerging markets, such as India, Indonesia, and Russia. Nissan chiefs confessed that the Datsun name still carried a reputation for value and reliability, more than 30 years after it had been scrapped. Datsun Go and Do models are now selling well in many countries, despite being badged with a rather neutral blue-and-silver version of the old logo.

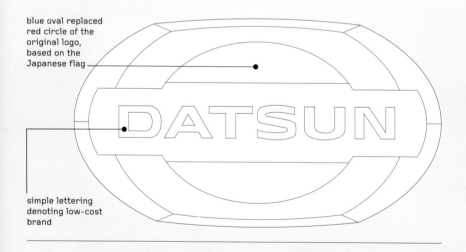

blue oval replaced red circle of the original logo, based on the Japanese flag

simple lettering denoting low-cost brand

000.000.000.030
#B3B3B3

085.075.000.000
#2640FF

000.000.000.100
#000000

DᴇLOREAN

FOUNDED
October 24 1975 (Detroit, USA)

FOUNDER(S)
John DeLorean

YEARS OF OPERATION
1981–1983

BEST-KNOWN MODEL
DMC-12

Only a few thousand of John DeLorean's ambitious stainless steel, gull-wing doored coupés were sold, and yet it retains a global fame out of all proportion with its success in the showroom. This was due to the uniqueness of the project, which was fronted by a colorful businessman and engineer who insisted on being buried in jeans and a motorbike jacket when he died in 2005.

The pioneering mid-engined Italian-designed car was built in the unlikely setting of Northern Ireland. In its short lifespan it generated worldwide interest. The company was brought down by financial problems, but the fame of the cars lived on.

The choice of a DMC for the *Back to the Future* movies sealed the car's celebrity status, but the badge also became iconic. The logo with its simple DMC block capitals mounted in the center of the narrow, horizontal front grille was designed by Detroit artist Phil Gibbon, who still calls it "my 15 minutes of fame." The corpulence of the letters demonstrates the corporate greed of the 1980s, but there's no denying that by losing the stem of the "D" on the logo the design has the immediacy and symmetry of a classic palindrome.

That's why the logo is still sold as badges and stickers all over the Internet today, more than 30 years after the company went out of business.

upright of the "D"
removed so that the
logo is symmetrical

initials stand for DeLorean
Motor Company

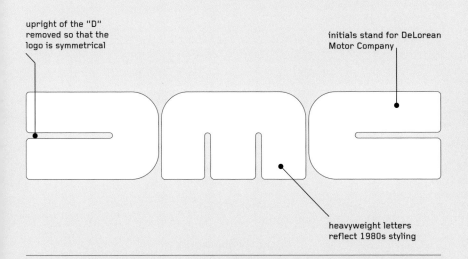

heavyweight letters
reflect 1980s styling

000.000.000.030
#B3B3B3

DODGE

FOUNDED
1900 (Auburn Hills, USA)

FOUNDER(S)
Horace Elgin and John Francis Dodge

YEARS OF OPERATION
1900–present

BEST-KNOWN MODELS
Viper, Charger, Challenger, Dart, Ram

You'll see today's logo on the front grille of most Dodge models. It's simply the word Dodge in neat capitals, finished with two red diagonal lines. It marks a very restrained point in the history of one of the USA's most changeable automotive badges.

This historic marque has a strong identity as a rugged performance brand. However, its emblem has been through a long list of incarnations since Dodge Brothers' engineering workshop adopted a fancy logo in the 1900s: the capitals "D" and "B" interlocked within two concentric circles. The circles later became a six-pointed star within blue circles. Soon there was also a distinctive hood ornament, originally a leaping ram, which later

became streamlined to just a ram's head, and finally just a pair of horns. This became a recurring emblem for Dodge trucks.

A traditional heraldic Dodge "family crest" appeared in the 1940s and was used intermittently. Dodge was also using the "Forward Look" twin boomerang logo of parent company Chrysler (see pages 54–55). Then followed 20 years of the "fratzog" triple arrowhead emblem, although this competed for hood space with the red Chrysler pentastar. Ram trucks, meanwhile, started using a ram logo again, while the Viper always used a snake's head badge. Confused? Perhaps that's why Dodge introduced its current low-key, simpler badge for its 2011 models.

simple design replaced
badges featuring company
name and ram's head logo ⸺

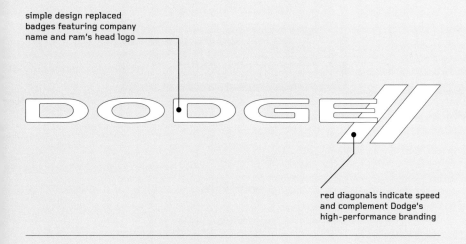

red diagonals indicate speed
and complement Dodge's
high-performance branding

000.000.000.030
#B3B3B3

000.090.080.000
#FF1933

FERRARI

FOUNDED
1939 (Modena, Italy)

FOUNDER(S)
Enzo Ferrari

YEARS OF OPERATION
1940–present

BEST-KNOWN MODELS
Dino, California, LaFerrari, F40, 250GTO, F355

Ferrari is one of the world's best-known marques, and its celebrated supercars wear one of the industry's most easily recognizable emblems: the famous prancing horse. To be more exact, Ferrari's badge is a black horse rearing on its hind legs above the word Ferrari, or the initials SF (Scuderia Ferrari), with three thin strips that represent the Italian flag along the top. The whole arrangement is usually mounted in a yellow shield or box.

The badge dates back to before the birth of Ferrari. Founder Enzo Ferrari was racing for Alfa Romeo in 1923 and met Countess Paolina, mother of Italian First World War aristocratic flying ace Francesco Baracca. She asked him to use a prancing horse on his car because it had been the symbol painted on the side of her son's biplane. The horse was probably used because Baracca had officially been a member of the Italian cavalry.

The emblem was supposed to bring good luck, although sadly the young airman was actually shot down and killed after 34 victorious duels. Eventually, the fiercely patriotic Ferrari adopted the "lucky" horse on his own racing cars and added a yellow background, the official color of the city of Modena near the Ferrari factory.

Today, the black horse on a yellow shield usually appears on steering wheel bosses and front wings, while the horse by itself is likely to adorn the hood and trunk.

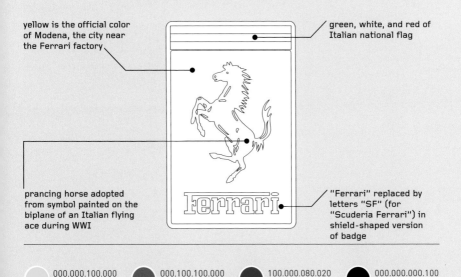

yellow is the official color of Modena, the city near the Ferrari factory

green, white, and red of Italian national flag

prancing horse adopted from symbol painted on the biplane of an Italian flying ace during WWI

"Ferrari" replaced by letters "SF" (for "Scuderia Ferrari") in shield-shaped version of badge

000.000.100.000
#FFFF00

000.100.100.000
#FF0000

100.000.080.020
#00CC29

000.000.000.100
#000000

Profile: ENZO FERRARI

NATIONALITY
Italian

BORN
February 18 1898 (Modena, Italy)

DIED
August 14 1988 (Maranello, Italy)

FOUNDER
Ferrari S.p.A

To everyone involved in the automobile industry and motor racing, Enzo Ferrari was not simply the founder of the company—he *was* Ferrari. A born salesman, obsessive, egocentric, and flamboyant, Ferrari the man was all about the racing. He realized early in his career that manufacturing road cars was the only practical way of financing his pricey racing activities, and in doing so managed to create some of the most exciting cars ever to grace a public highway.

Ferrari was born in Modena, in the Emilia-Romagna region of northern Italy, on February 18 1898. At the tender age of ten Enzo was taken to watch a motor race at the famous Circuit di Bologna. He was instantly hooked and resolved to become a racing driver. Following an unsuccessful application for driving work at Fiat in Turin, Ferrari was first offered a test-driving position at the Milan-based car manufacturer Costruzioni Meccaniche Nazionali before switching to the racing team at Alfa Romeo in 1920. He enjoyed a fair degree of success (and it was around this time that the famous prancing horse began to appear on his racing cars), but was badly affected by the death of driver Antonio Ascari in the 1925 French Grand Prix, and decided to retire from driving after his first son Dino was born in 1932. Focusing instead on the management side of the sport, he formed the hugely successful Alfa Romeo racing team known as Scuderia Ferrari.

The relationship with Alfa Romeo began to sour in the 1930s and the Scuderia Ferrari team was dissolved for a time, but Ferrari was nonetheless retained as sporting director. However, a disagreement with Alfa's management in 1939 prompted Ferrari to found Auto-Avio Costruzioni, a company that made parts for other racing teams. The Second World War saw his company forced to produce military equipment, but peacetime presented fresh opportunities and Ferrari S.p.A was formed in 1947.

Ferrari is the only team to have competed in every season of Formula One since its formation in 1950 (using the revived Scuderia Ferrari name) and it has been said that Enzo's finest moment was the first time a Ferrari won a Grand Prix, beating an Alfa Romeo at Silverstone in 1951. By the late 1960s financial pressures meant Ferrari needed a business partner to fund the racing activities, and in 1969 Fiat bought 50 percent of the company on the agreement that Enzo would retain independent control of the racing team. He stepped down as managing director of the road car division in 1971.

Enzo Ferrari was often accused of ruthlessness, encouraging inter-team rivalries between individual drivers, but he always publicly acknowledged the risks taken on behalf of the team and reportedly never got too close to his drivers for fear of how it would affect him personally in the event of any of them being killed while racing (and many were). He died on August 14 1988 in Maranello, a place he hardly ever left during his life except to attend the Italian Grand Prix at Monza.

FIAT

FOUNDED
1899 (Turin, Italy)

FOUNDER(S)
Giovanni Agnelli

YEARS OF OPERATION
1900–present

BEST-KNOWN MODELS
500, Panda, Uno, Punto

Fiat began making cars back in 1900 and has grown to become one of the world's biggest automotive manufacturing groups. The Fiat Chrysler Automobiles (FCA) empire now encompasses brands as diverse as Dodge and Maserati.

In the beginning, however, the name Fiat was a simple acronym for Fabbrica Italiana Automobili Torino, the Italian Automobile Factory in Turin.

Those four capitals have, of course, formed the basis of the marque's badges ever since. They have usually been set in a sans-serif font, which has art nouveau overtones, particularly in the angle of the "A." The letters' setting, meanwhile, has evolved alongside the trends in design fashion. The earliest Fiat badges,

for example, have ornate gilded plinths for the Fiat name. Fancy laurel wreaths soon emerged to frame the four letters.

By the 1930s, the silver "Fiat" stood stark and alone on a red box with a silver border. The shape of the box went through various evolutions until the 1960s, when a completely new badge took over. The four letters sat side by side, each in a blue slanted box. This version lasted for more than 23 years. In 1999, however, that was all changed again. This time the letters returned to their more traditional format, but within a blue roundel.

The most recent incarnation, from 2007, includes a thickly bordered red box for the four capitals in a style reminiscent of the 1930s.

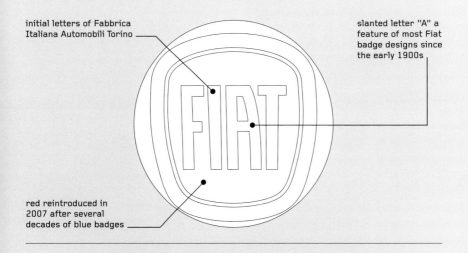

initial letters of Fabbrica Italiana Automobili Torino

slanted letter "A" a feature of most Fiat badge designs since the early 1900s

red reintroduced in 2007 after several decades of blue badges

000.000.000.030
#B3B3B3

025.100.045.010
#AC007E

000.000.000.100
#000000

FIAT: Evolution

Fiat's badges have always exhibited a certain Italian flair with their overtones of art nouveau. Over the years, the acronym "Fiat" has been the centerpiece but it has been mounted on a variety of roundels, shields, and boxes.

1904

1904

1921

1921

1921

1929

1932

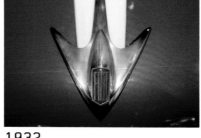

1932

1938

1959

1968

1991

FORD

FOUNDED
1903 (Detroit, USA)

FOUNDER(S)
Henry Ford

YEARS OF OPERATION
1903–present

BEST-KNOWN MODELS
Model-T, Mustang, Thunderbird, Fiesta, Escort, Taurus, Mondeo

Today, Ford's badge is so well known that the whole company is often referred to as "the blue oval," but it hasn't always been such a simple, recognizable emblem.

Back in 1903, when Henry Ford began his own car-making operation in Detroit, Michigan, design fashions were very different. So, his first choice of logo was a rather dainty presentation of "Ford Motor Co., Detroit, Mich" in a fashionably ornamental art nouveau border.

Within four years the branding had become a little more sophisticated. The badge became simply the script "Ford," thanks to staff designer Childe Harold Wills and his grandfather's stencil set. The neat graphic idea was used to adorn the radiator grille of the Model-T when it was launched the next year. For a short while the script sat on a blue winged pyramid before it was encased in an oval in 1912. By 1927, and the launch of the Model-A, the oval was blue, the script was white, and most of today's car-spotters would be able to recognize it immediately.

Later, there were a few slight experiments with the shape of the oval and some shading to add a three-dimensional touch, but essentially the badge on a global car such as today's Mondeo is much the same as it was before the Second World War.

oval shape introduced in 1912

script lettering created by Childe Harold Wills

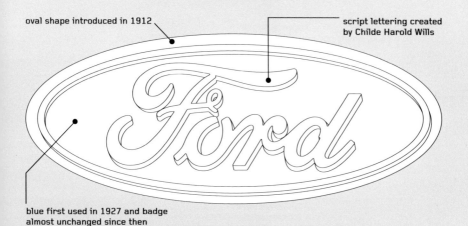

blue first used in 1927 and badge almost unchanged since then

 000.000.000.030
#B3B3B3

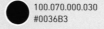 100.070.000.030
#0036B3

GAZ

FOUNDED
1932 (Nizhny Novgorod, Russia)

FOUNDER(S)
Soviet Union and Ford

YEARS OF OPERATION
1932–present

BEST-KNOWN MODELS
GAZ-M20, Volga, Chaika

For many years, vehicles from the GAZ car company were considered iconic symbols of the old Soviet era. The combination of imported American designs and technology with simple rugged Russian engineering created a range of sturdy, stately cars loved by party officials and coveted by those who were denied them.

However, GAZ is also a long-term industrial success story. The country's new communist leaders had kick-started an auto industry by importing millions of dollars' worth of Ford machinery and know-how to launch a car factory in 1932, originally called NAZ. Govky Avtomobilny Zavod (Gorky Car Factory) immediately began churning out clones of American cars. After the war, GAZ had gained the confidence to produce its own vehicles, which ranged from luxury cars to trucks. Around this time, an emblem of a leaping stag was introduced as a figure for the hood of the ZIM model. By 1981 the factory had produced its ten-millionth vehicle. Moving into the 21st century, GAZ concentrated on its successful truck business and stopped producing its own cars. Instead, foreign models are built under contract, while early GAZ cars have become sought-after collector's items.

Today, the GAZ badge still features the long-standing company symbol: a stag. This is mounted on a chrome-bordered shield with a red or black background depending on the model. The badge also contains the letters "GAZ" in Cyrillic script.

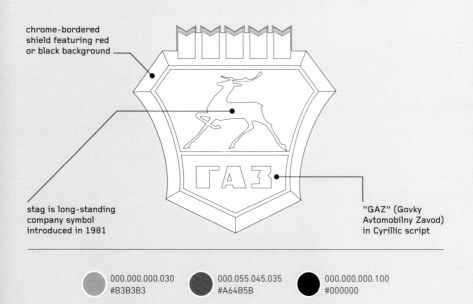

chrome-bordered shield featuring red or black background

stag is long-standing company symbol introduced in 1981

"GAZ" (Govky Avtomobilny Zavod) in Cyrillic script

000.000.000.030
#B3B3B3

000.055.045.035
#A64B5B

000.000.000.100
#000000

GMC

FOUNDED
1908 (Detroit, USA)

FOUNDER(S)
William C. Durant

YEARS OF OPERATION
1912–present

BEST-KNOWN MODELS
Yukon, Jimmy, Suburban, Terrain

You can tell from the bold red logo that GMC is a down-to-earth, no-nonsense brand. This is not the badge to be worn by a fragile supercar or exotic luxury limousine. That trio of bold scarlet capital letters with thick outline stands for the General Motors Truck Company, a division of the giant GM empire.

The GMC emblem wasn't always so forthright, however. The original prewar badge was a rather florid script with the stems of the "M" curling right under the two letters either side. The lettering was brutally simplified when marketing chiefs realized that wasn't really what truckers wanted. It wasn't sophistication that their customers were seeking, it was just the blunt, honest simplicity implied by three uncomplicated letters.

This marque first appeared back in 1912, on new trucks appearing at the New York Motor Show. It might have remained outside the scope of this book had it not later expanded into building pickups and SUVs. Today, however, it is a popular brand name for many big-selling family off-roaders and utility vehicles.

Within the colossal General Motors organization—which manufactures six marques and has nearly 400 facilities spread across six continents—there is plenty of rebadging of almost identical models to satisfy complex marketing requirements. You'll find that many GMC vehicles are actually identical to Chevrolet models—apart from that distinctive logo on the front grille that suggests the link with a truck-building company.

simple capitals emphasize
unpretentious nature of vehicles

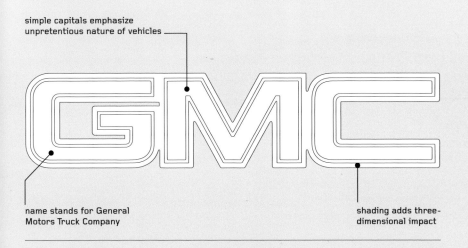

name stands for General
Motors Truck Company

shading adds three-
dimensional impact

000.000.000.030
#B3B3B3

000.090.075.000
#FF1940

Profile: WILLIAM C. DURANT

NATIONALITY
American

BORN
December 8 1861 (Boston, MA)

DIED
March 18 1947 (New York, NY)

FOUNDER
General Motors Company, Chevrolet

William Crapo "Billy" Durant was, to say the least, a colorful character, whose ultimate claim to fame is as the first automobile entrepreneur to create a system of multibrand car manufacturing. Born in Boston, Massachusetts, on December 8 1861, Durant's family wealth stemmed from his mother's side, she being the daughter of Michigan governor Henry H. Crapo. The young William flunked high school in order to work at his grandfather's lumberyard, and in 1885 founded the Coldwater Road Cart Company in Flint, Michigan, with Josiah Dort. An initial investment of $2,000 had, by 1890, turned into a $2-million business with the renamed Durant-Dort Carriage Company enjoying global sales.

Ironically, Durant was initially anti-car; he considered them to be dangerous and even forbade his daughter from riding in one. However, he was smart enough to realize that the way forward was not to reject cars, but to work toward improving safety, thus increasing their popularity with the general public. He began by investing in the struggling Buick Motor Company, purchasing a controlling interest and becoming their general manager in 1904. Pairing with Canadian entrepreneur Samuel McLaughlin, Durant built and sold Buicks on a cost plus basis and subsequently founded the General Motors Holding Company in 1908 using $500,000 of Buick stock. GM subsequently bought Buick outright, and quickly followed up with the purchase of Oldsmobile, Cadillac, and Oakland (known later as Pontiac), all of which were merged with GM. Durant even made a play for Ford in 1909, arranging a multimillion-dollar deal, but the banks ultimately refused terms and, losing faith, the GM board of directors dismissed Durant.

Although financially compromised, Durant set about building another GM-style company. He formed a partnership with the French racing driver Louis Chevrolet in 1911 after securing some additional funds (thanks in part to Samuel McLaughlin) and founded the Chevrolet company. However, Durant and Chevrolet didn't get on and disagreements meant Durant eventually bought Chevrolet out in 1914. Subsequently, enough GM stock was reacquired (again with McLaughlin's help) and Durant found himself back on top as director of GM in 1916, bringing Chevrolet into the mix. His second reign lasted until 1920, when he was once again ousted by the shareholders.

In his later years Durant traded extensively on Wall Street but on the infamous Black Tuesday (October 29 1929) he stood by the fatal theory that buying rather than selling would bolster public confidence in the market. Durant, like many others, went bust. He suffered a stroke in 1942, ending his career managing a bowling alley in Flint where it had all begun, and died in New York in 1947. Sadly, at the time he was planning on opening a string of bowling alleys, predicting the potential for cheap family entertainment in the postwar boom of the 1940s. If nothing else, he could always spot a good business proposition when he saw one.

GREAT WALL

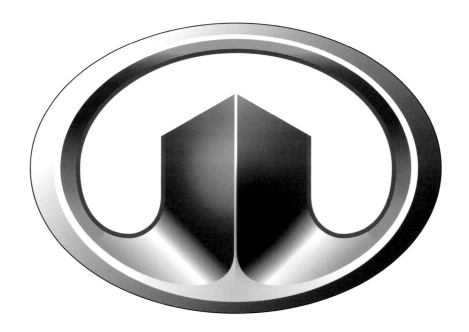

FOUNDED
1984 (Baoding, Hebei, China)

FOUNDER(S)
State-owned

YEARS OF OPERATION
1984–present

BEST-KNOWN MODELS
M4, C50, Haval H6, WEY

China's largest SUV and pickup truck manufacturer is based in Hebei and is, of course, named for the Great Wall of China. That's because the eastern end of the famous wall begins in the province.

Great Wall Motors is a comparative newcomer in the automotive world, but was the first Chinese motor company to appear on the stock market. It was launched in 1984, initially just producing trucks. Great Wall didn't make its first car until 2010. Incredibly, sales doubled year on year for four consecutive years.

Within six years the brand had grown so fast that it was selling more than a million vehicles a year globally. It has already established manufacturing plants in other countries around the world. This rapidly rising marque's badge is a distinctive graphic representation of the wall itself. The center of the emblem shows the simple shape of one of the watchtowers that occur regularly along the ramparts of the wall. That shape is built into a three-dimensional chrome oval.

The company has increasingly tried to differentiate its SUVs from its passenger cars and so has established a sub-brand, Haval, for the off-roaders. The latest Haval vehicles do not carry the Great Wall logo, just a simple emblem in the grille, which spells the name "Haval" in red capital letters.

The company chairman, Wei Jianjun, was ranked sixth richest man in China in 2014, according to *Forbes* magazine, and his military precision approach to running his factories is well reported.

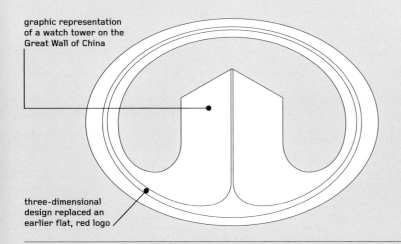

graphic representation of a watch tower on the Great Wall of China

three-dimensional design replaced an earlier flat, red logo

000.000.000.030
#B3B3B3

HINDUSTAN

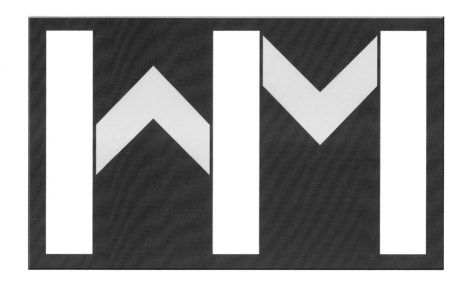

FOUNDED
1942 (Kolkata, India)

FOUNDER(S)
B. M. Birla

YEARS OF OPERATION
1942–present

BEST-KNOWN MODELS
Ambassador, Contessa

The Bengal-based Hindustan brand is one of India's most well-known automotive manufacturers. It was the country's first car-making company, established just before the country's independence thanks to a collaboration with the British Morris Motors company, and was the largest carmaker in India until the rapid rise of the Maruti Group.

For more than 50 years, Hindustan produced its own cars (loosely based on the template of the stately postwar Morris Oxford), most notably the brand's most famous model, the Ambassador. The Indian company has also made business agreements with Mitsubishi, Isuzu, and Peugeot to produce vehicles for them on the subcontinent.

The Hindustan Motors company emblem is a slightly complex graphic arrangement of an overlapping capital "H" and "M" in white and yellow on a blue square. In corporate settings this is generally shown with the company name beneath in blue capitals.

The renowned long-serving Ambassador, however, had its own emblems. It often used the "Ambassador" name in small chrome capitals across the front of the hood with a classic flying wing figure just above. Other Ambassador models sported a small chrome "H" on a red roundel with chrome wings either side. It remains a popular car for taxis in India and has its own cult following around the world.

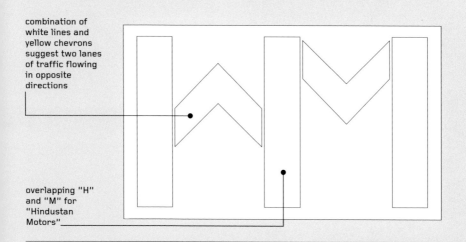

combination of white lines and yellow chevrons suggest two lanes of traffic flowing in opposite directions

overlapping "H" and "M" for "Hindustan Motors"

000.000.000.000
#FFFFFF

095.060.000.000
#0D66FF

000.000.100.000
#FFFF00

HOLDEN

FOUNDED
1856 (Adelaide, Australia)

FOUNDER(S)
James Alexander Holden

YEARS OF OPERATION
1856–2017

BEST-KNOWN MODELS
The Holden, Coupé Utility, FJ, Monaro, Commodore

Australia's best-known motoring brand was originally simply an Adelaide-based saddle maker. The company evolved into tackling the leather interiors of motorized carriages, repairs to bodywork followed, and by the end of the First World War James Holden was starting to make car bodies for foreign manufacturers to fit to imported chassis.

Holden's logo from this era was "the lion and stone" designed by sculptor Rayner Hoff. The emblem referred to a legend that the wheel was invented after men saw lions rolling stones.

When the Great Depression hit in 1931, one of the foreign importers, U.S. company General Motors (GM), stepped in and bought the struggling Holden. After the Second World War, GM launched Australia's first home-produced car. It was simply called The Holden. The logo was changed into a more modern graphic representation of a lion, which was certainly fiercer, too.

There followed a series of tough, powerful, and versatile models designed for the Australian market that proved to be immensely popular. Holden has continued to be a major part of Australian life with a sequence of home-grown and rebadged GM vehicles. Meanwhile, the Holden badge has been gradually reworked to become a distinctive motoring emblem, although still showing the lion with its stone.

In 2017, however, GM announced plans to close its Australian factories, marking the end of an era for car manufacturing in Australia.

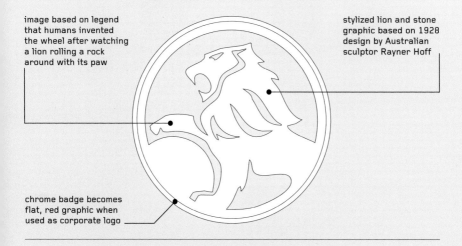

image based on legend that humans invented the wheel after watching a lion rolling a rock around with its paw

stylized lion and stone graphic based on 1928 design by Australian sculptor Rayner Hoff

chrome badge becomes flat, red graphic when used as corporate logo

000.000.000.030
#B3B3B3

HONDA

FOUNDED
September 24 1948 (Hamamatsu, Japan)

FOUNDER(S)
Soichiro Honda

YEARS OF OPERATION
1949–present

BEST-KNOWN MODELS
Accord, Civic, NSX, CR-V, Insight

With its name spelled out in its familiar red bold capital letters, Honda has grown to become a familiar brand around the world. Small wonder, because this major Japanese engineering company now makes a huge range of things, from jets to garden power equipment. The company was founded by former garage mechanic Soichiro Honda after the Second World War. At first, it grew slowly and the first automobile wasn't produced until 1963. After that the company took off, with exports to the West soaring. Honda was soon able to produce a wide range of vehicles, including mass-market hatchbacks, pioneering hybrid cars, and the NSX supercar.

Today, each division of the Honda company uses a different specialist logo. The automobile branch uses a simple chrome capital "H," while its luxury sub-brand Acura (see pages 16–17) uses a similar capital "A." The "H" obviously stands for Honda but was also selected because the clear letter shape appears equally recognizable in the West as in the East. It's a neutral typeface with no hint of Japanese calligraphy.

The design of the "H" has an element of subtlety, too: it is broader at the top than the base, implying a figure raising its arms to the sky. It perfectly complements the Honda slogan, "The power of dreams."

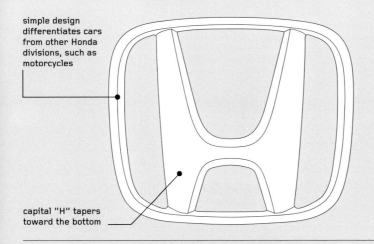

simple design differentiates cars from other Honda divisions, such as motorcycles

capital "H" tapers toward the bottom

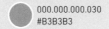

000.000.000.030
#B3B3B3

HUMMER

HUMMER

FOUNDED
1979 (Mishawaka, USA)

FOUNDER(S)
AM General

YEARS OF OPERATION
1992–2010

BEST-KNOWN MODELS
H1, H2, H3

The front badge makes it pretty clear: this is a bold, tough, and seriously purposeful vehicle. The style of the Hummer logo is certainly forthright and to-the-point. It simply consists of the word "Hummer" spelled out in fat black capital letters. There is no room for frills and artistry here, and that perfectly suited the vehicles that wore the Hummer badge.

The first prototype for the heavyweight brand was created by AM General for the U.S. military in 1980. In 1992 the company began marketing the Hummer to the public. It was trying to market a more civilized version of the hardcore Humvee military vehicle. The vehicle gained a lot of media interest, with celebrity Arnold Schwarzenegger being a high-profile fan.

General Motors bought the Hummer marque from AM General in 1999 and proceeded to build a sequence of three vehicles that got progressively less military and more civilized as sales plummeted. In the light of difficult economic conditions, and the horrific fuel consumption of the Hummers, production of the H3 stopped in 2009, and the brand has since disappeared (though the Humvee is still produced by AM General for the military market).

The vehicle badges for each of the Hummer models were as brutally simple as the marque's primary logo. They featured a large, fat capital "H," semi-overlaid with a similarly bold digit "1," "2," or "3." It wasn't pretty, but nobody was left under any illusions about what they were buying.

chunky capitals connote
rugged, utilitarian vehicle

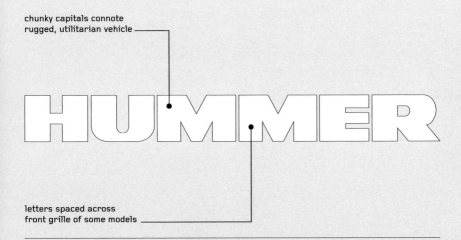

letters spaced across
front grille of some models

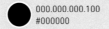

000.000.000.100
#000000

HYUNDAI

FOUNDED
1967 (Seoul, South Korea)

FOUNDER(S)
Chung Ju-Yung

YEARS OF OPERATION
1967–present

BEST-KNOWN MODELS
Santa Fe, Accent, Tucson, Coupe, i10

This Seoul-based company didn't start making cars until 1967. Chung Ju-Yung started the Hyundai Motor Company to build the Cortina in Korea, in association with Ford. In the 1970s Chung hired former Austin Morris boss George Turnbull to lead development of the first Hyundai car. In 1975 Hyundai produced South Korea's first mass-produced vehicle, the Hyundai Pony. A combination of great value and well-built cars quickly propelled the company into the top division of global automotive manufacturers, currently operating in more than 180 countries.

Hyundai's badge looks like a simple "H," the initial letter of the company name. At a casual glance, it seems a little similar to the Honda logo (see pages 98–99), and you might think a designer dreamed it up without much consideration. But, of course, multinational motor manufacturers apply much more sophisticated thought to the development of their logos.

Hyundai is a Korean word meaning "modernity." The hidden thought behind the apparently simple logo is that the stylized "H" sits within an oval, which symbolizes Hyundai as a worldwide company. Moreover, the letter is slanted to the right, suggesting progressive forward motion. Hyundai also suggest that the shape of the "H" implies two people shaking hands. One is a satisfied customer, while the other is, of course, a Hyundai salesman.

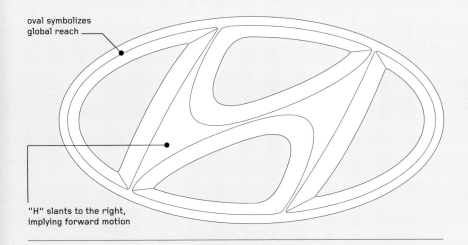

oval symbolizes
global reach

"H" slants to the right,
implying forward motion

000.000.000.030
#B3B3B3

INFINITI

FOUNDED
1989 (Tokyo, Japan)

FOUNDER(S)
Nissan Motor Co.

YEARS OF OPERATION
1989–present

BEST-KNOWN MODELS
Q45, Q60, QX30, QX70

When an elite group within Nissan decided to introduce a luxury vehicles division, one that would "challenge the prevailing American and European luxury brands with more human-centric design," they obviously spent many hours thinking about what to call it and what the logo should be. Details like that are crucial if you are badging vehicles in order to present them as belonging to a category elevated above your standard product.

Infiniti was finally chosen as the name to compete with upscale rivals such as Honda's Acura and Toyota's Lexus. It's a safe, neutral word that implies timelessness.

However, it's the brand's badge that has caused most debate among car-spotters. Nissan selected the now familiar combined chrome oval and pyramid shape. Different interpretations have been offered of what the badge represents. The first is that the central lines are stretching into the distance, symbolizing an infinite road. The second is that it is a mountain, specifically Mount Fuji in Japan, Nissan's homeland. Infiniti claims the mountain represents the summit of sophistication and technical progress. Infiniti has also compared the logo to the mathematical sign for infinity, which looks like a figure "8" on its side.

pyramid shape has been interpreted as a road stretching to the horizon or a graphic of Mount Fuji

overall design resembles the mathematical symbol for infinity

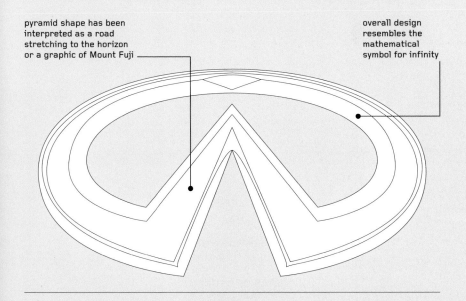

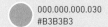

000.000.000.030
#B3B3B3

ISUZU

ISUZU

FOUNDED
1949 (Tokyo, Japan)

FOUNDER(S)
Yoshisuke Aikawa

YEARS OF OPERATION
1949–present

BEST-KNOWN MODELS
Trooper, Hombre, Rodeo, Piazza

Japanese manufacturer Isuzu is one of the world's largest truck makers, producing vast numbers of commercial vehicles and diesel engines, but there was a stage where it looked set to become one of the big car producers, too. In 1916, two Japanese industrial engineering companies jointly initiated plans for automobile production. In 1934, a Ministry of Trade and Industry standard model car was launched and named the "Isuzu," named for the river of the same name. This is the origin of the company name, which became Isuzu Motors Limited in 1949.

Isuzu's first passenger car, the Bellel, arrived in 1961. The company grew impressively. This persuaded GM to invest heavily in Isuzu in the 1970s and led to plenty of rebadging of Isuzu models within the GM global framework. Isuzu also

started producing popular SUVs, pickups, and cars, such as the innovative Piazza Turbo, introduced in 1985.

It was time for the old-fashioned company logo of a decorative shield to be completely updated. The result was two vertical pillars with slanting tops forming a graphic emblem. They are representations of the first syllable in the Japanese spelling of 'Isuzu'. It normally appeared in white on a red square with "Isuzu" spelt out in plain capital letters beneath.

Later, however, as the company became more focused on trucks and engines, the logo was simplified. The Isuzu badge today features the company name in capitals. There is subtlety in the typography, though—the "S" and "Z" are identical mirror images.

simple capitals connote
functional, efficient vehicles

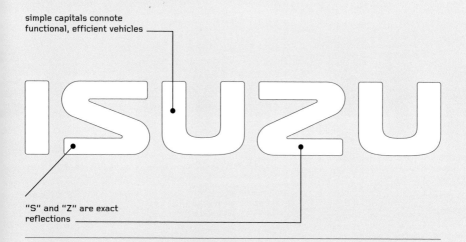

"S" and "Z" are exact
reflections

000.000.000.030
#B3B3B3

JAGUAR

FOUNDED
1922 (Coventry, UK)

FOUNDER(S)
William Lyons

YEARS OF OPERATION
1935–present

BEST-KNOWN MODELS
E-Type, XK120, XJ220, XJS, F-Type

In the 1920s, this grand British sports icon actually started off making motorcycle sidecars. The company then progressed to car bodies and eventually complete cars. The Jaguar brand name was adopted in 1945 and it has gone on to become a worldwide prestige car builder, now owned by an Indian conglomerate.

The leaping jaguar figure was added to the hoods of the cars after the Second World War as an attempt to create a distinctive and stylish emblem. The jumping predator epitomized the grace, performance, and power that Jaguar was trying to achieve with its sports cars. As fashions (and safety rules) changed, the little hood statue became a graphic logo. Until 2002 the animal was a sketched outline. Ford, which took ownership of the company in 1990, added shading to the figure. The latest Jaguar badge, designed by current owners Tata, resembles a sleek metallic leaping jaguar seen from the side, its menacing jaws open and teeth bared. The figure is shaded with gray and black to give it a three-dimensional appearance. The marque name is spelled out underneath in capitals using a fatter, squatter new font, and they too have a three-dimensional treatment.

The badge everyone most associates with the marque now appears on the rear of the latest cars. The front grille badge is a more conventional emblem: a roundel with the face of a jaguar in silver on a red background and a silver surround featuring the word "Jaguar."

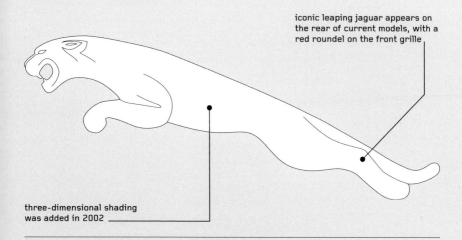

iconic leaping jaguar appears on the rear of current models, with a red roundel on the front grille

three-dimensional shading was added in 2002

000.000.000.030
#B3B3B3

JEEP

FOUNDED
1941 (Toledo, Ohio)

FOUNDER(S)
John North Willys

YEARS OF OPERATION
1941–present

BEST-KNOWN MODELS
Cherokee, Wrangler, Patriot, Compass

The Jeep brand dates back to the famous versatile military vehicle that played such a practical role for the Allies in the Second World War. After the war, the rights to produce this basic four-wheel-drive utility vehicle were handed over to Willys, one of the main companies that had produced wartime jeeps. Various basic civilian versions were launched, but none with much success.

After several buyouts and takeovers, the brand name ended up in the hands of Chrysler (see pages 54–55) in 1987. It was around the time of the launch of what some would consider the first proper new vehicle since the basic jeep, the Wrangler. The Jeep marque has stayed within the Chrysler stable ever since, although Chrysler itself has now become part of the Fiat (see pages 80–83) empire.

Although the thick vertical stripes of the traditional military jeep's radiator grille are still part of the modern Jeep brand identity, today's automotive marketing departments prefer to have a graphic logo as well. It allows them to add a marketing device to everything from websites to baseball caps.

Given the unfussy and practical nature of the brand's vehicles, it's probably no surprise that Jeep uses an unpretentious design for its vehicle badge and logo. It's just the word "Jeep," presented without a background and in a very simple typeface.

brushed steel with green outline

simple, functional design complements reputation for robust vehicles

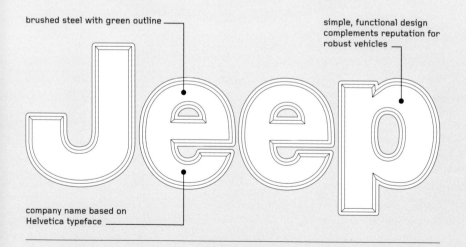

company name based on Helvetica typeface

000.000.000.030
#B3B3B3

KIA

FOUNDED
1944 (Seoul, South Korea)

FOUNDER(S)
Chul-Ho Kim

YEARS OF OPERATION
1944–present

BEST-KNOWN MODELS
Sorento, Sportage, Soul, Rio

Kia Motors Corporation gives its founding date as 1944. The name is a combination of two symbols meaning "arising from Asia." The company initially produced bicycles. The first car wasn't built until 1974, and even then progress was slow because the Korean government insisted that Kia concentrate on building trucks. The company developed its first car in 1986. Early models such as the the Pride/121 and Festiva used technology licensed from Mazda and Ford, but the bodies were designed by Kia. Just as it began to grow its exports, Kia was hit by a financial crash and this resulted in a partnership with Hyundai. Kia has recovered strongly, but remains part of the Hyundai Group.

Kia now operates under the slogan "The power to surprise," perhaps in order to dispel suspicions created in some people's minds by its somewhat cheap and cheerful early products. The marque's current badge (designed by Peter Schreyer) is deceptively simple: the company name in capitals on an oval roundel. The missing horizontal bar on the "A" lends it visual interest and a slightly futuristic aura. Unusually, Kia uses a completely different badge in its home market. Korean Kias wear an emblem that is a distinctive "K" with a double upright stem on a blue circle within a black ring containing the words "Kia Motors." It's a more dynamic logo, but is reserved for home customers.

corporate logo is red, but car badge is generally chrome with a black background

missing bar on "A" adds interest and creates a futuristic vibe

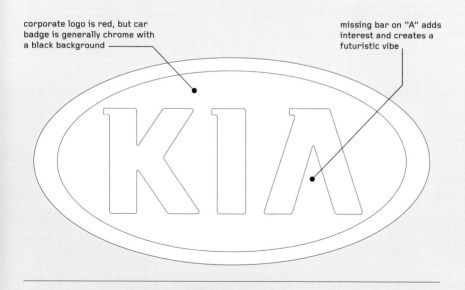

005.100.080.025
#B60026

KOENIGSEGG

FOUNDED
August 12 1944 (Ängelholm, Sweden)

FOUNDER(S)
Christian von Koenigsegg

YEARS OF OPERATION
1994–present

BEST-KNOWN MODELS
CCX and Agera

Swedish entrepreneur Christian von Koenigsegg had a definite aim when he founded his car company in 1994: to build a world-class supercar. From his small factory in Olofstrom, Sweden, it only took him six years. By 2009, experts were judging the Koenigsegg CCX one of the most beautiful cars ever made. His cars also offer extraordinary performance. It's impressive that such a small operation could break the record for the world's fastest production car, breaking the lap time for the benchmark Nürburgring test track (Agera).

In addition, the company (which is now based in Ängelholm) has won praise for its pioneering steps in both technology and environmentalism. One of Koenigsegg's most headline-grabbing inventions has been a new material using carbon fiber coated with diamond dust that shimmers in the light. The CCXR Trevita features this material for its bodywork, and as a result is one of the most expensive production cars ever made.

The company badge was created right at the start by von Koenigsegg's close friend, graphic designer Jacob Låftman (who has sadly since died). The Koenigsegg motif is based on the coat of arms of the von Koenigsegg family, which dates back 900 years to an ancestor who was knighted by the Holy Roman Emperor, Charles VI. It features yellow and red diamonds on a blue-bordered shield. The graphic device at the top of the shield is a clever combination of the letters "KCC."

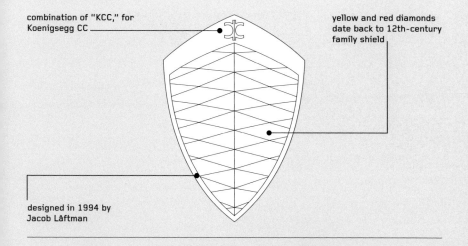

combination of "KCC," for Koenigsegg CC

yellow and red diamonds date back to 12th-century family shield

designed in 1994 by Jacob Låftman

 010.025.100.000
#E6BF00

000.075.080.010
#E6392E

 100.080.000.020
#0029CC

LADA

FOUNDED
1970 (Tolyatti, Samara Oblast, Russia)

FOUNDER(S)
State government

YEARS OF OPERATION
1970–present

BEST-KNOWN MODELS
Riva, Nova, Signet, Niva

The symbol of Lada has always been what people in the West assumed to be a Viking-style longboat with a dragon's figurehead and a billowing sail propelling it forward. However, it actually shows a Russian "ladya," a similar shallow-drafted historic riverboat.

The badge itself has been through different incarnations, just like the company. The best-known era of Lada cars was the 1980s, when the brand's owners, Russian industrial group AvtoVAZ, exported its cheap, basic vehicles to the West. The factory was alongside the Volga River, hence the riverboat link.

Names of models varied among Lada's target markets. The design was based on an old Fiat but the badge was pure contemporary Russian. It was a red upright oblong with a stylized white sailing ship. In retrospect, it was a fine badge considering the car was often ridiculed in the press for its unsophisticated quality.

Lada was a big earner of foreign currency for the Soviet Union. Other models followed, notably the likable little Niva off-roader of 1978 that was a cult success across much of the world, apart from the USA. This basic, rugged 4x4 is still built today.

The Lada brand retreated from many developed markets but still operates at home and in some parts of South America and Asia. Its cars still wear the "ladya" badge though, with the riverboat heading to the right and enclosed in an oval border.

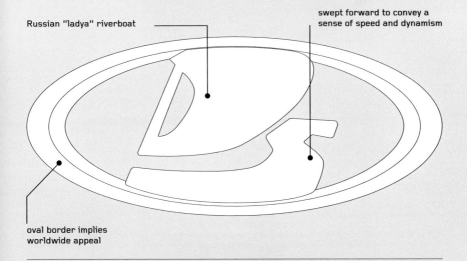

Russian "ladya" riverboat

swept forward to convey a sense of speed and dynamism

oval border implies worldwide appeal

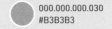

000.000.000.030
#B3B3B3

LAMBORGHINI

FOUNDED
1963 (Sant'Agata Bolognese, Italy)

FOUNDER(S)
Ferruccio Lamborghini

YEARS OF OPERATION
1963–present

BEST-KNOWN MODELS
Countach, Diablo, Gallardo, Aventador, Huracan

Tractor producer Ferruccio Lamborghini was a rural engineer who was always rather fond of bulls. His star sign was Taurus and he was fascinated by the Spanish sport of bullfighting. In 1962, Lamborghini visited a renowned fighting-bull ranch near Seville in Spain, which was owned by Don Eduardo Miura. This family ranch had been breeding the fiercest fighting bulls since 1842.

The next year, Lamborghini opened a car-making business and chose one of Miura's fighting bulls as the emblem of his new enterprise. Of course, we know now that the company went on to become one of the biggest names in high performance supercars. And Lamborghini would name many of his cars after famous bulls. He even named one for Don Eduardo and his breed of bulls.

The Lamborghini badge was designed in the light of this passion for bulls. It depicts a gold bull on a black shield with the company name in simple capitals. It's a distinctive logo and one that Lamborghini probably intended as something of a repost to his big local rival Ferrari (see pages 76–79), who used similar colors and a similarly agitated farm animal. Of course, it also allows Lamborghini, which is now under the control of Audi, to claim that its badge represents features of the bull, such as power, strength, and bravery.

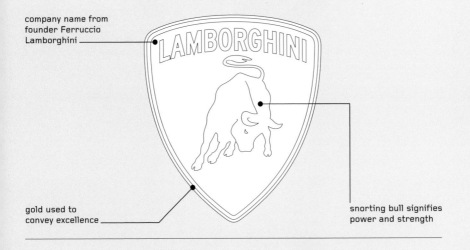

company name from founder Ferruccio Lamborghini

gold used to convey excellence

snorting bull signifies power and strength

000.020.080.000
#FFCC33

000.030.100.020
#CC8F00

000.000.000.100
#000000

LANCIA

FOUNDED
November 29 1906, Turin, Italy

FOUNDER(S)
Vincenzo Lancia

YEARS OF OPERATION
1906–present

BEST-KNOWN MODELS
Delta, Stratos, Beta

Car badges were not always the vital marketing tools they are today. When Vincenzo Lancia started building cars in the early part of the last century, he didn't bother with a marque badge at all. A discreet brass plaque identified the maker and chassis number.

Years earlier, Lancia had befriended an aristocratic artist, Count Carlo Biscaretti di Ruffia. In 1910 he belatedly asked the Count to come up with ideas for a badge for his cars. Ruffia returned with a series of artistic watercolors. The one chosen showed the name "Lancia" in gold on a blue flag attached to a lance. In Italian, *lancia* means "lance." The whole motif was laid on top of a four-spoke steering wheel.

In 1929, reverting to another of Ruffia's drawings, the badge was placed onto a blue shield, and during the 1950s and 1960s the Lancia emblem was refined to an open chrome design with the flag at the center. In the 1970s, the logo reverted to the shield badge in time to appear on the famous Delta range. It stayed in this traditional form until 2007.

At the time, Lancia's sporting and luxury heritage was being downplayed by parent company Fiat. The badge was correspondingly simplified to a chrome-framed blue shield with the word Lancia, but without the lance or flag, though spikes at the top and bottom of the central silver circle do allude to the original lance.

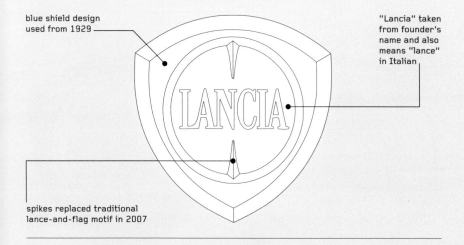

blue shield design
used from 1929

"Lancia" taken
from founder's
name and also
means "lance"
in Italian

spikes replaced traditional
lance-and-flag motif in 2007

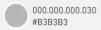 000.000.000.030
#B3B3B3

 100.090.000.000
#0019FF

LANCIA: Evolution

With the exception of the earliest calligraphic marque, the development of Lancia's marque has been relatively subtle. The four-spoke steering wheel, lance and flag have only recently been rationalised to a simpler design.

1907

1911   1929

1957

1974

2000

2007

LAND ROVER

FOUNDED
1978 (Coventry, UK)

FOUNDER(S)
British Leyland

YEARS OF OPERATION
1978–present

BEST-KNOWN MODELS
Defender, Discovery, Freelander, Range Rover

The original spartan and versatile Land Rover appeared just after the Second World War. Its badge was similarly basic and utilitarian. The black roundel contained the words "Land Rover" in capitals, with "Solihull, Warwickshire" alongside, denoting where it was built.

In 1978 British Leyland made Land Rover a standalone company and vehicles were given the luxury of a model identification plate under the badge. This simply said something like "Defender 110", with space left for the serial number. It wasn't until 1989 that a green oval was used. It still only said "Land Rover," but the previous rough line connecting the words "Land" and "Rover" had grown into something of a motif.

The addition of more luxurious consumer vehicles to the basic Land Rover model forced logo designers to constantly push the badge more upscale. Modern Land Rover emblems are still simple, emphasizing the practical nature of the vehicles, but with a neat modern serif typeface implying a certain level of class.

Land Rover went through various owners before joining Jaguar as part of India's Tata Motors. The latest badge is still unfussy: the oval contains the brand name and the two linking squiggles. The oval is shaded to give a three-dimensional touch. Its distinctive green, somewhat unusual for a car badge, emphasizes the off-road abilities of the vehicles.

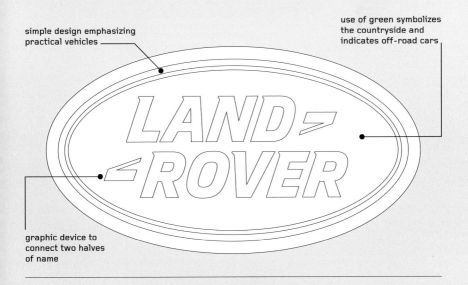

simple design emphasizing practical vehicles

use of green symbolizes the countryside and indicates off-road cars

graphic device to connect two halves of name

000.000.000.030
#B3B3B3

090.030.090.020
#148F14

LEXUS

FOUNDED
1989 (Nagoya, Japan)

FOUNDER(S)
Eiji Toyoda

YEARS OF OPERATION
1989–present

BEST-KNOWN MODELS
LS400, IS300, RX300, SC430

Toyota ambitiously launched a separate brand to market its luxury vehicles in 1989. The company tried to launch the new marque by building "the best car in the world." The high-tech super-smooth LS400 limousine came pretty close to their target.

At the same time, the Japanese carmaker was careful to ensure the marketing was perfectly fine-tuned. Adverts were handed to top agency Saatchi & Saatchi. Lippincott & Margulies consultancy was given the job of coming up with an upscale, globally recognizable name, while Molly D. Designs and Hunter Communications were employed to create a logo. Firstly, the list of possible names was narrowed down to "Alexis," which was gradually refined through meetings and clinics to "Lexus." Meanwhile, designers produced a simple but elegant badge featuring a capital "L" within a chrome oval. Company representatives have claimed that it was the result of a very precise mathematical formula, although details of the formula have never been divulged.

Somehow, this simple graphic conjured an image of stylish affluence and futuristic technology. Interestingly, however, the "L" in the badge is nothing like the "L" in the name of the company that usually appears alongside it, which also uses a custom typeface drawn up specially for Lexus. The car, the name, and the badge all worked their magic, and Lexus has become a major upscale automotive brand across the world.

stylized capital "L" within chrome oval creates a simple yet elegant design

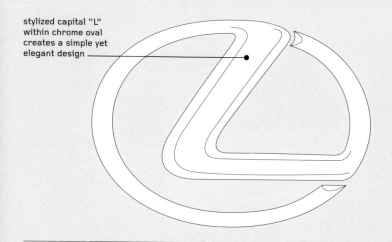

000.000.000.030
#B3B3B3

LINCOLN

FOUNDED
1917 (Dearborn, Michigan, USA)

FOUNDER(S)
Henry Leland

YEARS OF OPERATION
1917–present

BEST-KNOWN MODELS
Continental, Town Car, MK

In 1917, engineer Henry Leland named his new car company after the first politician he had voted for, way back in the 1860 presidential election. After financial problems, Ford took over Lincoln in 1922 and launched the most famous model, the Continental, in 1940. This was based on a one-off luxury custom car created for Henry's son, Edsel, in 1939.

Leland was also the founder of the Cadillac brand and so was influential in creating two of America's most luxurious marques. Since then, Lincoln has kept its branding rather straightforward. In the early Ford years a greyhound figure was fixed to the hood. By the 1930s, Lincolns wore a badge of a red cross topped by a knight's helmet, loosely based on a medieval crusader's cross. Like the cars, this device became more decorative during the 1950s but gradually evolved into a more streamlined and simplified logo featuring a simple framed cross. At various times, for differing promotional purposes, this graphic has enabled it to be likened both to a compass and a star.

Appropriately, given the origin of the name, Lincoln became the vehicle of choice for many U.S. presidents. A convertible 1961 Lincoln Continental will forever be remembered as the car in which President Kennedy was assassinated. Ford relaunched the brand, however, in the early 2000s as The Lincoln Motor Company, aiming to reposition the marque in the global marketplace and appeal to young buyers of other luxury marques. Since then, sales have reportedly been growing steadily in the US and there is now a substantial market for the marque in China.

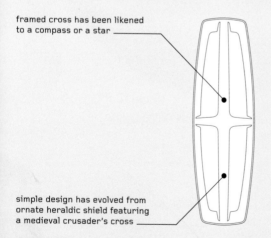

framed cross has been likened to a compass or a star

simple design has evolved from ornate heraldic shield featuring a medieval crusader's cross

000.000.000.030
#B3B3B3

000.000.000.100
#000000

LOTUS

FOUNDED
1952 (Norwich, UK)

FOUNDER(S)
Anthony Colin Bruce Chapman

YEARS OF OPERATION
1952–present

BEST-KNOWN MODELS
Seven, Elan, Esprit, Elise

This specialist sports car manufacturer was founded by the British inventor and engineer Anthony Colin Bruce Chapman in 1952. Although Chapman was normally known as Colin, the overlapping four initial letters of his name form the center of the Lotus badge. The initials and the brand name stand on a triangle of the traditional motorsport color, British Racing Green, within a yellow circle, symbolizing the sunny days Chapman believed lay ahead.

A company legend about the original badge hints at Chapman's maverick character. It is said that he led his original financial partners, Michael and Nigel Allen, to believe that the letters stood for Colin Chapman and the Allen Brothers. The name Lotus, meanwhile, was believed to have been chosen because Chapman's pet-name for his wife Hazel was "my Lotus flower."

In 1968 the colors of the badge were replaced with a black background. This was intended as a temporary tribute to British World Champion Formula One driver Jim Clark, who died racing in a Lotus. The chaotic Lotus parts division occasionally used up stocks of these black badges randomly over the following years. Some enthusiasts believe these "black-badged" cars had up-rated performance or engines.

The black badge was also used after the death of founder Chapman in 1982. The company then went through several owners with corresponding branding changes. For a while, Chapman's initials were dropped and the badge changed to a gold marque name on a green oval. None of the new varieties seemed to work, though, and eventually the traditional Lotus badge was restored.

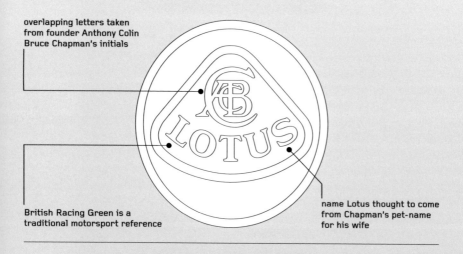

overlapping letters taken from founder Anthony Colin Bruce Chapman's initials

British Racing Green is a traditional motorsport reference

name Lotus thought to come from Chapman's pet-name for his wife

 000.000.000.030
#B3B3B3

 000.005.090.000
#FFF219

 085.020.100.070
#0B3D00

MAHINDRA

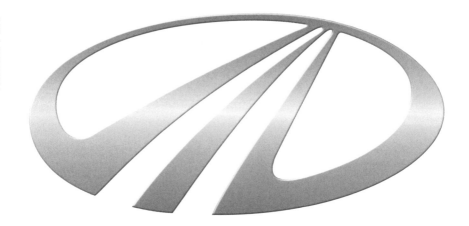

FOUNDED
October 1945 (Mumbai, India)

FOUNDER(S)
Jagdish and Kailash Chandra Mahindra and Ghulam Mohammed

YEARS OF OPERATION
1945–present

BEST-KNOWN MODELS
Jeep, Scorpio, Bolero, Xylo

One of India's biggest motoring manufacturers started life as a steel company established by two brothers and Ghulam Mohammed, who left in 1947 to become finance minister of the newly formed Pakistan. In the early years, Mahindra & Mahindra started making versions of the wartime Willys Jeep, then later expanded to include vans and agricultural vehicles.

The company has become one of the subcontinent's great commercial successes. It now produces cars, motorcycles, and electric vehicles and has taken over Korean manufacturer SsangYong. It builds vehicles in India, China, Brazil, the UK, and the USA.

The company is part of the enormous group Mahindra Rise, a multinational that engages in activities as diverse as aerospace and insurance.

Mahindra is a Hindu name, meaning king or god. The automotive division's logo, however, is a little more humble. The graphic badge can either be seen as a sloping capital "M" encased in a circle or a road stretching away to the horizon. This is the chrome symbol that appears at the center of the front grille of all the models, from the long-standing all-Indian Scorpio SUV to the Verito family sedan, a rebadged Dacia Logan.

Until now, Mahindra has maintained separate brand identities between its own vehicles and the SsangYongs from Korea. Both appear with their own marque badges, but there are reports that Mahindra may be about to demonstrate the flexible nature of today's automotive branding world by badging Ssangyong models with Mahindra logos for the Indian market.

design could be capital "M" or road leading ahead

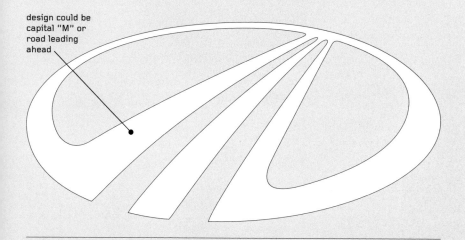

000.000.000.030
#B3B3B3

MASERATI

FOUNDED
December 1 1914 (Bologna, Italy)

FOUNDER(S)
Alfieri, Ettore, and Ernesto Maserati

YEARS OF OPERATION
1914–present

BEST-KNOWN MODELS
Ghibli, Quattroporte, GT

There is a distinctive emblem mounted on the front grille of every Maserati. The iconic trident badge that instantly identifies this classic Italian marque is a copy of part of a classical statue that stands in the central Piazza Maggiore in Bologna, the company's original home city. The bronze statue of Neptune is a 16th-century Renaissance masterpiece by Giambologna, and part of a landmark fountain in the city.

Following the war, the fledgling motorsport company acquired the trident badge in 1920. One of the seven Maserati brothers, artist Mario, wasn't involved with the formation of the new company, but did have a lasting impact on its branding when he used part of the nearby statue for the company's logo. The trident was a proud local symbol and the brothers thought it would portray strength and vigor.

The company has since grown into a classic Italian exotic carmaker with a glamorous reputation around the world. Maserati is now part of the giant group Fiat Chrysler Automobiles. It has even moved from Bologna to the nearby city of Modena. However, through all this upheaval the Maserati badge has remained much the same as Mario's original design. The version shown here is red on a white and blue oval, but in recent models the trident symbol often appears as a simple chrome device on the front grille.

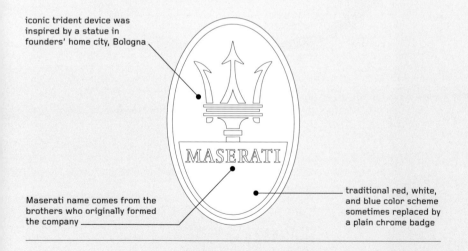

iconic trident device was inspired by a statue in founders' home city, Bologna

Maserati name comes from the brothers who originally formed the company

traditional red, white, and blue color scheme sometimes replaced by a plain chrome badge

000.000.000.000
#FFFFFF

000.100.100.005
#F20000

075.055.000.050
#203980

MAZDA

FOUNDED

January 30 1920 (Hiroshima, Japan)

FOUNDER(S)

Jujiro Matsuda

YEARS OF OPERATION

1929–present

BEST-KNOWN MODELS

Mx-5/Miata/Eunos, RX-7, Bongo, CX-5

Like most motor manufacturers, Japanese company Mazda has a separate corporate logo and car badge. The logo is the word "Mazda" written in a mix of blue capitals and lowercase letters, with a distinctively split "Z" in the center. You'll still find this on company documents, but in the 1970s and 1980s this simple nameplate was used as a badge on all Mazda vehicles, including the first generation of the hugely popular MX-5/Miata/Eunos range of two-seater roadsters, which appeared in 1989.

The company introduced a more graphic emblem in 1991. This design, known as the cylon logo, showed a ring within an oval frame that loosely referred to the rotary engines that have been uniquely used in Mazda vehicles such as the RX-7 sports car. The badge had to be hastily redesigned within a year, however, because Mazda chiefs realized it was confusingly similar to the contemporary Renault emblem.

In 1997, as Ford took a controlling interest in the financially troubled company, a completely new emblem appeared. The chrome badge that has adorned the front end of all the company's vehicles ever since is an elegant pair of flying wings within an oval. The design can also be seen as a letter "M" within an oval frame. The Ford/Mazda partnership was broken in 2015 but the company has retained the now familiar "wings" logo.

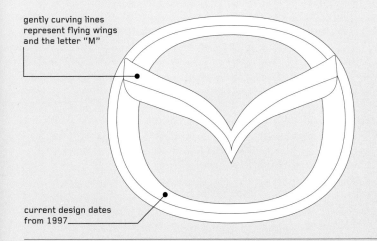

gently curving lines represent flying wings and the letter "M"

current design dates from 1997

McLAREN

FOUNDED
1963 (Woking, Surrey, UK)

FOUNDER(S)
Bruce McLaren

YEARS OF OPERATION
1963–present

BEST-KNOWN MODELS
F1, P1, 675LT

The high-performance lightweight sports cars produced by the small British company McLaren feature specialist technologies from the company's heavy involvement in motorsport. That's because the Surrey-based company was originally purely focused on the track. It wasn't until 1988 that it set out to create a road-going supercar. The resulting carbon-fiber three-seater F1 was one of the most advanced and distinctive sports cars in the world, but it appeared to be a one-off project with a limited run of just 106 cars. After that, McLaren waited until 2010 to return to the road-going world. It returned for good this time and has launched a range of high-end sports cars that has enabled it to become established.

McLaren has one of the simplest yet most individual (and therefore memorable) badges in this book. The company had used various badges and emblems over the previous 50 years of racing, but they realized there's a big difference between a team emblem and the logo for an upscale supercar. Previous jaunty designs, including a New Zealand Kiwi bird, were ditched in favor of a stylish rendering of the company name in a neat, modern font, placed in a rectangle with rounded corners. Alongside the name is a slightly mysterious crescent symbol. The "swoosh" design implies movement and speed, and, according to McLaren itself, is a graphic interpretation of "the vortices created by our rear wing."

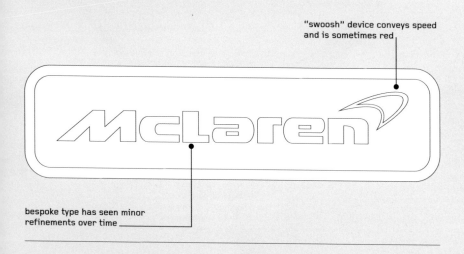

"swoosh" device conveys speed and is sometimes red

bespoke type has seen minor refinements over time

000.000.000.030
#B3B3B3

000.000.000.100
#000000

MERCEDES-BENZ

FOUNDED
June 1926 (Stuttgart, Germany)

FOUNDER(S)
Names

YEARS OF OPERATION
1926–present

BEST-KNOWN MODELS
Motorwagen, C-Class, SL, G-Wagen, 300 SL Gull-wing Coupe, S600, SLS, M-Class

The three-pointed Mercedes star is often judged the most recognizable trademark in the world, yet the star device doesn't date back to the start of the company. Mercedes can trace its origins back to Karl Benz's 1886 Motorwagen, the first gas-powered car, and one engineer who named an early car for his daughter Mercedes in 1901—but it wasn't until 1926 that companies DMG and Benz & Cie combined forces to establish the Mercedes brand.

When he was still alive Daimler had patented a three-pointed star and this was combined with the Benz laurel circle to create their first badge. Daimler's star had evolved from humble origins: it was the mark he once made on a postcard to show someone where his house was.

This strong graphic emblem became the symbol of the prestigious German marque. At first it was a simple star decorating radiators. The circular frame came later. From the 1920s onward, however, design chiefs had the brilliant idea of mounting the star in a circle on the front of the hood. It became an instantly recognizable symbol that lasted until the end of the 20th century, when concerns about the danger of accidents with pedestrians forced a change.

Mercedes models now retain this iconic logo by featuring a large encircled star as an integral part of the design of the front of all models, from the humble A-Class hatchbacks and commercial vans to the GT supercar and SL luxury flagships.

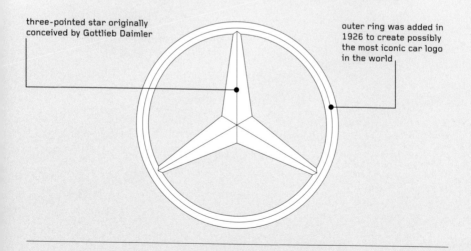

three-pointed star originally
conceived by Gottlieb Daimler

outer ring was added in
1926 to create possibly
the most iconic car logo
in the world

000.000.000.030
#B3B3B3

Profile: GOTTLIEB DAIMLER

NATIONALITY
German

BORN
March 17 1834 (Schorndorf, Germany)

DIED
March 6 1900 (Stuttgart-Bad Cannstatt, Germany)

FOUNDER
Daimler Motors Corporation

The pioneering designs of Gottlieb Daimler (third from the left in the photo, opposite) and his lifelong business partner Wilhelm Maybach paved the way for the engines that power practically every car on the road today. He and Maybach (whose input to the development of the modern internal combustion engine equals Daimler's) both worked for the Cologne-based engineering firm Deutz, and it was here that Daimler was inspired to rethink how the large, stationary four-stroke engines designed by Deutz's co-owner Nikolaus Otto could be adapted for use in vehicles.

The differences between Daimler's early engine designs and those of Otto were slight, centered mainly around the ignition system and thus creating potential patent issues. Daimler's contract at Deutz was terminated in 1880, but the courts ultimately found in Daimler's favor and he was able to continue his work. Maybach resigned his own position and returned to work with Daimler once again.

Otto's engines used gaseous fuel and were designed as an alternative to steam engines, but this system was not ideal for Daimler's smaller engines, so he and Maybach decided that petroleum was the way to go. In 1883, they patented their first engine which ran on ligroin, a petroleum distillate which had been used mainly as cleaning fluid. The engine was compact and fast-running (for the time) at 750 rpm, the two main goals Daimler had set. Further design innovations were subsequently added, including an electronic ignition system designed by Bosch, which replaced Daimler's earlier hot-tube system.

In 1885 the pair built the Reitwagen (riding car), a wooden framed motorcycle and the first vehicle powered by an internal combustion engine. Maybach managed to reach a maximum speed of 7.5 miles (12 kilometers) per hour on a two-mile (three kilometer) test ride. They followed this up in 1886 by installing a larger version of the same engine in a coach body, creating the first four-wheeled "automobile." However, a couple of months earlier and just 60 miles (96 kilometers) away in Mannheim, the engineer Carl Benz had succeeded in building and patenting a self-powered three-wheeled vehicle, the Benz Patent Motor Car. Subsequently, Benz is regarded as the inventor of the first automobile.

Daimler and Maybach produced several more vehicles, including the 1889 Stahlradwagen, and founded Daimler Motoren Gesellschaft on November 28 1890 with backing from several wealthy industrialists. The Mercedes three-pointed star originates from this period and symbolizes Daimler's wish to create engines that could power vehicles on land, on water and in the air. Unfortunately, Daimler was unable to maintain full control of his company, ultimately forcing his decision to resign from DMG soon after its formation.

Daimler died on March 6 1900 after suffering from heart problems for several years. Because of their differences over various claimed patent violations and general rivalry, he and Carl Benz never met or indeed ever spoke to one another, but on June 28 1926 DMG and Benz & Cie merged to form Daimler-Benz, of which Mercedes

MERCURY

FOUNDED
1938 (Detroit, USA)

FOUNDER(S)
Edsel Ford

YEARS OF OPERATION
1938–2011

BEST-KNOWN MODELS
Grand Marquis, Sable, Monterey, Capri, Cougar

While the logos of individual motor manufacturers are a vital part of marketing, the emblems of sub-brands created by a manufacturer are even more important. Badge-engineering, or simply renaming models from a different marque, has long been a part of the auto industry. Distinctive brand logos are essential for this, because they may signify the only difference between the models. Ford created its new, moderately upscale marque in 1938 after considering more than 100 different names. Most of the models sold during Mercury's 73-year history were renamed, redesigned, or revamped Ford models, often with the slight addition of chrome and nicer seats.

The first badge selected to represent this new brand, which was intended to sit in the market somewhere between standard Fords and luxury Lincolns, was a portrait of the Roman god Mercury wearing his speed-enhancing winged hat. This classical motif also sometimes functioned as a hood ornament. However, in the boom times of the 1950s, a new, more modern Mercury emblem appeared, known as "The Big M." As the name suggests, this was a capital letter "M" with long horizontal bars extending either side.

The final Mercury badge appeared in the more challenging marketplace of the 1980s. It seemed to be a graphic representation of the winged helmet, with three silver bent lines within a double roundel. Despite the more modern badge, Mercury sales continued to fall in the 21st century. The last model was produced in 2011.

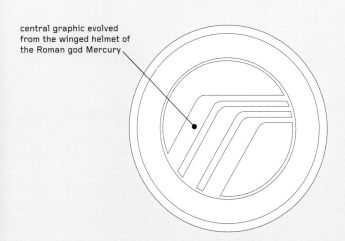

central graphic evolved from the winged helmet of the Roman god Mercury

000.000.000.030
#B3B3B3

000.000.000.100
#000000

MG

FOUNDED
1924 (Oxford, UK)

FOUNDER(S)
Cecil Kimber

YEARS OF OPERATION
1924–present

BEST-KNOWN MODELS
MGA, Magnette, MGB, Bullnose Morris, Midget

One of the classic marques of the golden era of British motor manufacturing, MG started as a prewar sideline for a showroom called Morris Garages in Oxford. The garage began selling its own versions of some of the Morris vehicles produced by its owner, William Morris (later Lord Nuffield) in 1924. These were adapted to be a little sportier than the standard cars. To emphasize the differences between the garage's own cars and the Morris originals, they were branded as MGs.

Business grew and the simple octagonal badge containing the letters "MG" was registered as an official trademark by Morris Garages in 1924. The specialist sports-car producer succeeded at first, producing acclaimed cars like the Magnette and the MGA. However, MG was gradually swallowed up by larger conglomerates.

Having already merged with Austin in 1952, MG became part of British Leyland Motor Corporation (BLMC) in 1968, which had already acquired Triumph in 1960. Within BLMC, the MG marque became simply used for badge-engineered (rebadged) versions of other marques (such as Austins), with the exception of the MG sports cars.

As part of the MG Rover Group, which was formed in 2000, the MGF, an all-new roadster, was launched. However, only five years later, the company went into administration and was purchased by NAC, China's oldest carmaker. The new owners have tried to revitalize the old brand, introducing a completely new range of cars, such as the MG6, but retaining the traditional octagonal badge and the initials of the long-disappeared garage in Oxford.

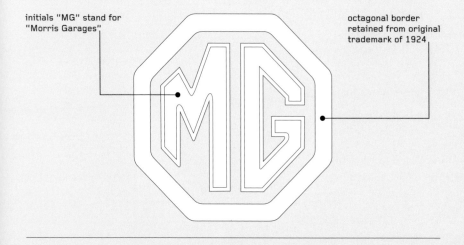

initials "MG" stand for
"Morris Garages"

octagonal border
retained from original
trademark of 1924

MINI

FOUNDED
1959 (Oxford, UK)

FOUNDER(S)
Sir Leonard Lord, head of British Motor Corporation (BMC)

YEARS OF OPERATION
1959–present

BEST-KNOWN MODELS
Mini Cooper

Unlike the majority of contemporary car marques, the Mini brand is built around a single car, the iconic Mini designed by Alec Issigonis and launched in April 1959. Issigonis had previously worked on design projects for Humber, Morris Motors, and Alvis before returning to the British Motor Corporation (BMC), a company formed by the merger of Morris Motors and the Austin Motor Company in 1952.

Initially, the Mini was marketed under the separate Morris and Austin brands. The Morris version was known as the "Mini" or alternatively the "Morris Mini-Minor," referencing the slightly larger Morris Minor model that the company continued to produce. Austin's version was initially to be called the Austin Newmarket but was eventually named the Austin Seven as a nod to their famous Austin 7 model from the 1920s and 1930s. The separate brands finally combined to become a single marque in 1969.

The brand is now owned by BMW and the current badge has been in continuous use since 2001. It uses a cleaner, more modern version of the logo for the first high-performance Mini Coopers and retains the central circular device with silver wings, designed to express a sense of speed and freedom. The limited color palette helps provide a feeling of quality and excellence.

A minimal version of the logo in plain black and white, designed by Berlin-based firm KKLD, appears online and in all promotional material.

upper-case lettering and black background retained from Mini logo of 1969

stylized wings adapted from Mini Cooper badge of 1962

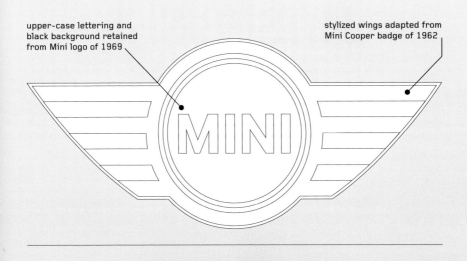

000.000.000.030
#B3B3B3

000.000.000.100
#000000

MITSUBISHI

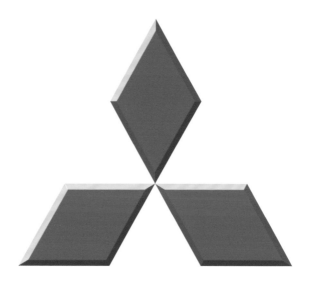

FOUNDED
1870 (Osaka, Japan)

FOUNDER(S)
Koyata Iwasaki

YEARS OF OPERATION
1870–1946 and 1952–present

BEST-KNOWN MODELS
Eclipse, Lancer, Montero, 3000GT

Mitsubishi is descended from an industrial conglomerate founded by Yataro Iwasaki in 1870. The Mitsubishi Shipbuilding Company, which formed part of the conglomerate, began making cars in 1917, thanks to Yataro's nephew, Koyata Iwasaki, who was the company's fourth president. The Mitsubishi Model A carries the distinction of being Japan's first series-production car.

The overall business grew to become Mitsubishi Heavy Industries, which was Japan's largest company until it was disbanded during the occupation of Japan in the aftermath of the Second World War. In 1952, the company was allowed to reform and began building buses, trucks, and Willys Jeeps. By the 1960s Mitsubishi had become one of the driving forces in the fast-growing Japanese motor industry. It has acquired a reputation for advanced technology. Today it is a globally known marque and part of the Renault-Nissan-Mitsubishi Alliance.

The company's name is drawn from a combination of two words: *mitsu*, meaning three, and *hishi*. *Hishi* literally means "water chestnut," but it has long been used to denote a diamond shape. When the two words are combined, the "h" of *hishi* is pronounced as a "b," hence Mitsubishi.

The logo design of three red diamonds was chosen by Yataro Iwasaki. It cleverly combines the three-leaf crest belonging to the Lords of Tosa, Iwasaki's first employers, with the Iwasaki family's own emblem, formed from three vertically stacked rhombuses. The company name and the logo together form a key part of Mitsubishi's brand identity. There is little wonder that it has survived unchanged for so long.

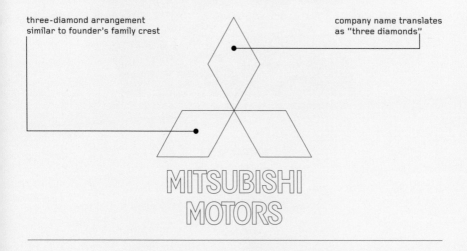

three-diamond arrangement
similar to founder's family crest

company name translates
as "three diamonds"

MITSUBISHI
MOTORS

000.100.100.000
#FF0000

000.000.000.100
#000000

Profile: YATARO IWASAKI

NATIONALITY
Japanese

BORN
January 9 1835 (Aki, Tosa Province, Japan)

DIED
February 7 1885 (Edo, Japan)

FOUNDER
Mitsubishi

Great success is sometimes born from political and social upheaval, as was the case with Yataro Iwasaki. Born into a provincial farming family in 1835, Iwasaki began his career working for a group of merchants, the Tosa Clan, whose business involved the export of specialty goods such as camphor and bonito flakes, a kind of dried skipjack tuna used in traditional Japanese cooking. They also imported warships and other types of military equipment.

Iwasaki was the Clan's trading operations manager in Nagasaki, which at that time was the only port authorized by the government to operate commercially outside of Japan. However, Japan's Western trade links were undergoing a rapid rate of expansion around that time and in 1869 Iwasaki successfully relocated much of the Clan's operation to Osaka, increasing business and profits considerably. A holding company, Tsukumo Shokai, was established by the Clan in 1870, but clan rule was abolished in Japan in 1873 and Iwasaki was able to take full control of the company, renaming it Mitsubishi Shokai. Iwasaki had quickly established himself as one of the most powerful businessmen in Japan.

By 1874, the company had relocated once again, this time to Tokyo, and was renamed Mitsubishi Jokisen Kaisha. The company's principal contract sold and leased ships to the Japanese government—Mitsubishi owned an incredible 73 percent of the total gross tonnage of Japan's fleet of steamships at that time—and many were used by the Japanese military to transport troops to areas of unrest during the 1870s.

Like many of the industrialists who would help shape the automobile industry in the future, Iwasaki's principal contribution to the development of Mitsubishi was to encourage diversification. Copper mining was just one of the areas that Iwasaki exploited, opening up previously untapped resources through the introduction of new technology. Other industries added to the Mitsubishi empire included coal mining, warehousing, and exchange services, and ship building and repair after Mitsubishi leased and later purchased the ailing Nagasaki Shipyard in 1884. The company also established the Tokio Marine Insurance Company, the first general (or nonlife) insurance company to exist in Japan.

Iwasaki was known for his lavish and expensive dinner parties, with guest lists composed of major dignitaries and government officials. This clearly helped to cement the company's reputation and secured its future success, which Iwasaki was unfortunately not able to enjoy as he died from stomach cancer in 1885. One has to wonder what he could have done with car manufacturing, given a few extra years.

MUSTANG

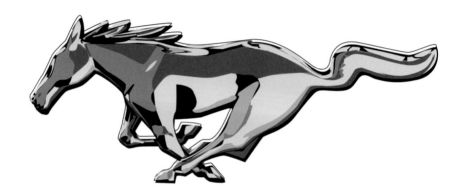

FOUNDED
1964 (Dearborn, Michigan)

FOUNDER(S)
Ford

YEARS OF OPERATION
1964–present

BEST-KNOWN MODELS
n/a

When a customer focus group was asked which was the best name for a forthcoming new "special car," Cougar was the favorite. Prototypes already wore cougar badges but Henry Ford wanted "T-Bird." "Torino" was also popular. At the last minute, marketing chief Robert Eggert, a horse-lover, added "Mustang" to the list. To everyone's surprise, it was voted the winner.

In 1964, Ford's new car appeared: a two-door, two-plus-two seater with a long sporty hood and short sloping "fastback." The Mustang wasn't just a sales success, it provided the template for a new class of automobiles known as pony cars, and inspired scores of muscular-looking coupés.

Ford designers had been sketching possible badge designs since 1962. The logo had to combine the speed of a galloping horse with an indisputable sense of an all-American product. Much discussion followed about whether it should face left or right. Eventually a striking wooden carving by sculptor Charles Keresztes was chosen and a chrome version fixed to the grille of the new car.

The American manufacturing was emphasized by mounting the horse in other places around the car on a red, white, and blue strip. Ford expected to build 100,000 Mustangs a year, but more than a million were sold in the first 18 months. The car has gone on to become an American motoring icon, with starring roles in movies like *Bullitt*, *Diamonds are Forever*, and *Need for Speed*. The sixth generation Mustang, manufactured in Flat Rock, Michigan, continues to sell well around the world and each new version is instantly recognizable—thanks to the galloping horse on the front grille.

design based on
wooden carving of
galloping horse

000.000.000.030
#B3B3B3

NISSAN

FOUNDED
1934 (Tokyo, Japan)

FOUNDER(S)
Yoshisuke Aikawa

YEARS OF OPERATION
1934–present

BEST-KNOWN MODELS
Sunny, Skyline, Leaf, Primera, X-Trail, Qashqai

The Nissan Motor Company is actually a large multinational corporation that also includes the recently resurrected Datsun and the luxury Infiniti auto brands. Here, we focus on the badge for Nissan, the company's mass-market brand. You may wonder why, however, because on the surface it's one of the least interesting logos to be featured in this book: it is simply the word "Nissan" in capital lettering on a chrome bar across the center of a circle.

Most independent observers would say the latest version of the Nissan emblem is very basic indeed. The badge's evolution, however, tells a more interesting story of the company's history. Nissan's in-house-designed cars were originally branded as Datsuns, the use of which name was preferred to distance the Nissan factory's association by U.S. customers with Japanese military manufacture. The first Datsun badge featured the brand name in a blue bar superimposed on a red sun, which reflected the Japanese national flag. When Datsun was dropped as the company brand name, the name Nissan simply took its place in the blue bar.

As Nissan looked to modernize its image, the colors were dropped and the badge became a graphic chrome representation of the original design. According to the company's marketing chiefs, this emphasizes the modern, sophisticated direction of more recent Nissan products, including the Leaf, the world's best-selling electric vehicle.

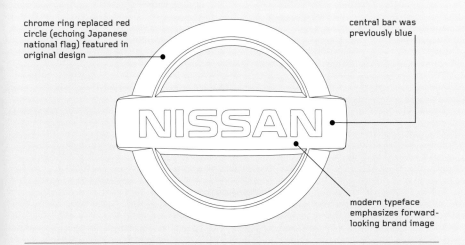

chrome ring replaced red circle (echoing Japanese national flag) featured in original design

central bar was previously blue

modern typeface emphasizes forward-looking brand image

000.000.000.030
#B3B3B3

000.000.000.100
#000000

OLDSMOBILE

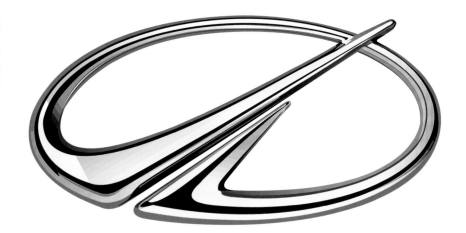

FOUNDED
1897 (Lansing, Michigan, USA)

FOUNDER(S)
Ransom Olds

YEARS OF OPERATION
1897–2004

BEST-KNOWN MODELS
Curved Dash, 442, Toronado, Cutlass, Aurora

Pioneering Michigan engineer Ransom Olds founded the Olds Motor Company in 1897, making it one of the world's first car manufacturers. In those early days, Olds produced steam, gas, and electric automobiles, and created one of the world's first car-assembly lines. The products rolling out of the factory soon became known as Oldsmobiles.

At the time, Olds' first car badge was a charmingly decorative design typical of the period, featuring the company name on a scroll across an ornate shield. However, Oldsmobile's independence didn't last long. By 1908 it was part of the General Motors empire, where it remained for the rest of its 107-year history. During this time the enduringly popular marque built more than 35 million vehicles.

Oldsmobile's badges changed completely over the generations, as design trends came and went. Prewar cars carried a complicated emblem, cramming elements including a winged spur, three acorns, the lamp of knowledge, and a micrometer into one crest. After the Second World War, the badge featured one of the most exciting symbols of the era: a rocket circling the earth. This was followed in the 1960s by a graphic representation of a rocket.

Finally, in 1996, GM switched the insignia once more. The new logo was in the style of the new Japanese car companies: a circle with a diagonal slash across it, described by the company as "a soaring rocket with a gentle oval." Sadly, Oldsmobile sales did the opposite of soar and the marque was retired in 2004.

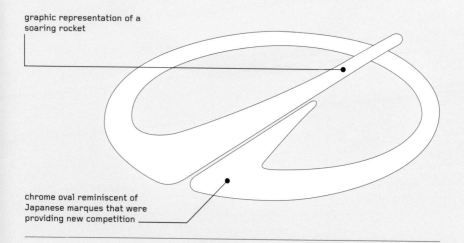

graphic representation of a
soaring rocket

chrome oval reminiscent of
Japanese marques that were
providing new competition

000.000.000.030
#B3B3B3

OPEL

FOUNDED
January 1862 (Rüsselsheim, Hessen, Germany)

FOUNDER(S)
Adam Opel

YEARS OF OPERATION
1862–present

BEST-KNOWN MODELS
Kadett, Rekord, Ascona, Manta, Vectra

Adam Opel's company began by making sewing machines, before anyone in the world had built an automobile, and by the 1880s was an established bicycle builder. Motorcycles and then, finally, in 1889, cars followed. Today Opel has become a brand offering a range of vehicles, from sports cars to panel vans. The company badge followed this evolution. Starting out with a florid 19th-century design using the founder's initials "A" and "O," this later became a more sober nameplate featuring the slogan "Victoria Blitz." "Victoria" was a reference to victory and *blitz* is the German word for "lightning," which was to become an important part of the Opel identity.

An early manufacturing success, dating from before the First World War, was the "Doktorwagen," an agile two-seater aimed at wealthy middle-class buyers like doctors.

General Motors, of America took over Opel before the Second World War and by the 1970s, due to GM's global strategy, its range was virtually the same as the British GM offshoot Vauxhall (see pages 208–209). For example, the Opel Ascona was virtually the same as the Vauxhall Cavalier, and the Opel Kadett was the Vauxhall Astra. There was also plenty of overlap with Holden (see pages 96–97), GM's Australian operation.

The early use of the word "lightning" influenced the Opel logo that appeared in the 1960s: a distinctive horizontal bolt. Gradually this was tidied to become a jagged symbol on a circular ring, which is the familiar modern Opel badge.

The French PSA group bought Opel from GM in the summer of 2017 and the company has announced that a change to the badge will be introduced in 2018.

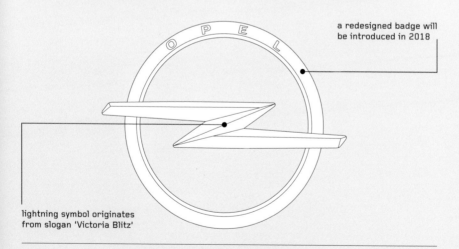

a redesigned badge will be introduced in 2018

lightning symbol originates from slogan 'Victoria Blitz'

000.000.000.030
#B3B3B3

PAGANI

FOUNDED
1992 (Modena, Italy)

FOUNDER(S)
Horacio Pagani

YEARS OF OPERATION
1992–present

BEST-KNOWN MODELS
Zonda, Huayra

Argentine engineer Horacio Pagani left his job at Lamborghini to set up his own specialist supercar operation in nearby Modena, Italy. It took a lot of borrowed money and many years of work, but eventually he was able to unveil his own car, the Zonda.

This ultra-lightweight mid-engined supercar was produced in small numbers for very affluent customers from 1999 to 2017. It was succeeded by Pagani's only other product, the Huayra.

This is another race-bred hypercar, which in 2013 was the fastest car round the BBC's *Top Gear* test track, when the quoted top speed was an extraordinary 238 mph (383 kph). The limited edition of 100 cars was sold out by 2015, which was good news for Pagani, considering they cost at least $1 million each. A second limited run of 100 roadster versions was announced in 2017—and, despite price tags of almost $2.5 million, they all promptly sold, too.

Pagani customers are perhaps not the sort who crave a conservatively designed global logo—the name and performance of the car is generally enough for them— which might explain why the company's badge design seems a slightly mysterious affair. The word "Pagani" stands in the center of an oval of drilled alloy, with "Automobili Modena" set beneath. The top-left corner has a flash of blue and an arrangement of lines that appear to form part of a letter "P."

Like every aspect of these finely hand-built cars, the badge is one of the most carefully crafted items in this book. Each one takes 24 hours to create, as it is carved from a solid block of aluminum.

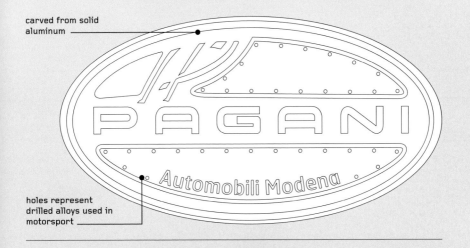

carved from solid aluminum

holes represent drilled alloys used in motorsport

000.000.000.030
#B3B3B3

100.070.000.000
#004DFF

PERODUA

FOUNDED
1993 (Serendah, Malaysia)

FOUNDER(S)
Daihatsu and various other Malaysian and Japanese partners

YEARS OF OPERATION
1992–present

BEST-KNOWN MODELS
Nautica, Axia, Bezza, Kembara

Malaysia's biggest motor manufacturer is highly unusual in that it didn't commission its own logo. Instead, in 1997 the company organized a national competition, open to anyone, to design a new badge.

Student architect Johnson Ng Weng Kuan from Kuala Lumpur won the contest and his design was promptly turned into the new company badge to be fitted to all 200,000 Peroduas built each year. It was launched with a fanfare to coincide with the unveiling of the new Kembara, Malaysia's first home-produced SUV (albeit a local version of the Daihatsu Terios).

For those unfamiliar with this Southeast Asian manufacturer, Perodua concentrates on building smaller, budget cars and SUVs. Current models include the Alza MPV, Axia hatchback, and Bezza sedan. The company has been building vehicles since 1993. It has a simple formula: it either uses components sourced from Daihatsu to create its own or it simply rebadges existing Daihatsu models.

Early Peroduas used a prancing deer logo. That was changed to a rather old-fashioned square design containing a big green "P" and a red background. The new competition-winning emblem is a more stylish, fluid, chrome oval with a central bar that hints at the letter "P" and creates dynamic shapes that retain the company colors.

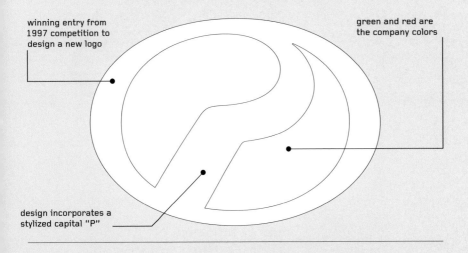

winning entry from 1997 competition to design a new logo

green and red are the company colors

design incorporates a stylized capital "P"

000.000.000.030
#B3B3B3

080.000.100.000
#33FF00

000.095.095.000
#FF0D0D

PEUGEOT

FOUNDED
1896 (France)

FOUNDER(S)
Armand Peugeot

YEARS OF OPERATION
1896–present

BEST-KNOWN MODELS
204, 504, 205 GTi, 406, RCZ

The origins of Peugeot can be traced back to 1810, when the Peugeot brothers started a company making coffee grinders. Bicycles followed and by 1896—following an encounter between Armand Peugeot and Gottlieb Daimler (pages 142–143)—the long-established French family business became one of the pioneers of car manufacturing and design.

The familiar badge on the front of all Peugeot vehicles today is a modern, three-dimensional graphic representation of a rampant lion. This logo has a history almost as long as the company. The lion first made an appearance in 1847, when Peugeot brothers Jules and Emile asked a jeweler to produce an emblem for their products. The resulting engraving, by Julien Blazer, featured a stately lion standing on

the shaft of an arrow. This emblem soon made its way onto Peugeot's steel tools, saw blades, coffee mills, bicycles, and motorcycles. By 1906 the lion appeared on its cars, too. In the 1920s Peugeot radiator caps were topped with lion figures. On successful prewar models, such as the 402, the lion's head became integrated into the front of the radiator—a slight move toward aerodynamics and safety.

The lion has appeared on generations of Peugeot models, from the boxy 403 of the 1950s to today's sleek 408 sedan. A more heraldic upright lion appeared on Peugeot trunk lids in the 1940s, then later migrated to the front grille of the cars. The lion in outline arrived with the 604 in 1975 and has gradually evolved to form a more fluid design.

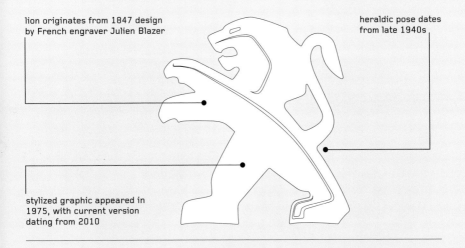

lion originates from 1847 design
by French engraver Julien Blazer

heraldic pose dates
from late 1940s

stylized graphic appeared in
1975, with current version
dating from 2010

000.000.000.030
#B3B3B3

PEUGEOT: Evolution

There's an obvious theme running through the evolution of the Peugeot emblem. The lion has changed dramatically, though, from the elegant beast of the 19th century to today's more rampant heraldic creature.

1905

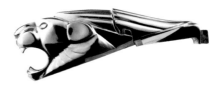

1933

1948

1955

1960

1968

1975

2008

PONTIAC

FOUNDED
1926 (Detroit, USA)

FOUNDER(S)
General Motors (GM)

YEARS OF OPERATION
1926–2010

BEST-KNOWN MODELS
Firebird, Trans Am, Bonneville, GTO

When General Motors (GM) wanted to create a new brand to fill the gap between its budget marques Chevrolet and Oakland, it chose the name of the heroic 18th-century Native American warrior chieftain who fought against the British. Something about the brand caught the public imagination and it soon outsold Oakland, which was hastily retired. Postwar models such as the Chieftain, Pathfinder, and Star Chief continued the Native American theme. All Pontiacs carried a badge or hood ornament featuring a Native American headdress, until this was replaced by a simple and more modern red arrowhead emblem in 1959.

Chrome strips running down the center of the hood were another Pontiac trademark and, in some cases, these ran from the back bumper to the front grille. These disappeared around 1957, but were replaced by a distinctive split-grille design that continued across the range until the end of their production in 2010.

In the 1960s Pontiac released some of its best-loved cars, such as the GTO and Firebird muscle cars. Star appearances in television shows, such as *The Rockford Files* and *Knight Rider*, helped elevate the Firebird's appeal, as did the brave decision to decorate the 1973 Trans Am model's hood with a full-sized image of a Native American "firebird." Eventually Pontiac became a victim of GM's financial struggles. While trimming jobs, dealers, and costs, GM dropped the Pontiac brand in 2010, although it still retains rights to the name and the arrowhead logo.

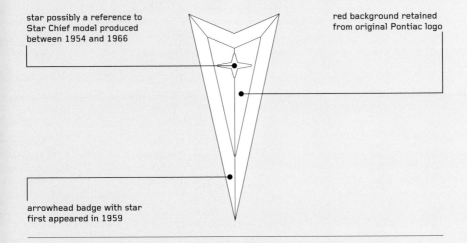

star possibly a reference to Star Chief model produced between 1954 and 1966

red background retained from original Pontiac logo

arrowhead badge with star first appeared in 1959

000.000.000.030
#B3B3B3

010.100.060.000
#E60066

PORSCHE

FOUNDED
1948 (Stuttgart, Germany)

FOUNDER(S)
Ferdinand Porsche

YEARS OF OPERATION
1948–present

BEST-KNOWN MODELS
911, Boxster, Cayenne

On April 25 1952 Ferry Porsche was in a New York restaurant with Max Hoffman, the U.S. importer for Porsche. Ferry, the son of Porsche founder Ferdinand, sketched the first draft of the possible Porsche crest on a paper napkin. The napkin later found its way to Porsche designer Franz Reimspiess, who had previously designed the Volkswagen logo in 1937 (see pages 212–213). Reimspiess had also been working on the unusual engine that sat in the back of these small Bavarian sports cars. Using Ferry's sketch, Reimspiess produced an emblem that was made to adorn the 356 rear-engined coupé of the time, but is still used on all Porsches to this day, from the Cayenne performance SUV to the iconic 911, the long-standing rear-engined successor to the 356.

The logo has an enduring appeal, symbolizing the heritage of Porsche and its roots in southern Germany. At the center of the gold crest is a smaller shield of yellow with a black prancing stallion, which echoes the coat of arms of the city of Stuttgart, where the company was founded in 1931. This is surrounded by stripes in the red-and-black colors of the Württemberg-Hohenzollern region (1945–53). The frilly motifs in the upper-left and lower-right quadrant are stylized antlers, which also appeared on the region's coat of arms. The name "Porsche" is added as a final seal across the top, making the whole design look like a medieval heraldic device, though in reality it sprang from that inspired doodle on a restaurant napkin.

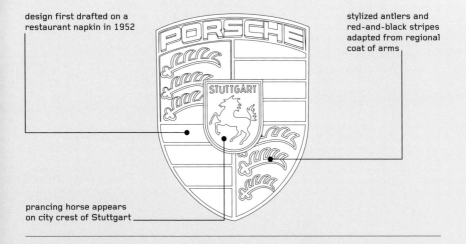

design first drafted on a restaurant napkin in 1952

stylized antlers and red-and-black stripes adapted from regional coat of arms

prancing horse appears on city crest of Stuttgart

000.010.085.000
#FFE626

015.100.080.005
#CE0030

000.000.000.100
#000000

PROTON

FOUNDED
May 7 1983 (Selangor, Malaysia)

FOUNDER(S)
State government

YEARS OF OPERATION
1983–present

BEST-KNOWN MODELS
Saga, Persona, Satria, Ertiga

The name Proton is an acronym loosely based on the company's full name Perusahaan Otomobil Nasional Sdn Bhd (National Automobile Company). Launched in 1983, it was at that time the only car producer in Malaysia, although Perodua (see pages 164–165) has since joined in. Initially Proton simply rebadged old Mitsubishi (see pages 150–153) imports from Japan. Nevertheless, some effort went into creating a badge to make the cars seem immediately Malaysian. Cars were given a blue emblem featuring a gold 14-pointed star and crescent moon, both national symbols of Malaysia.

Later Proton began to make more changes to Mitsubishi's designs and create its own models, such as the Waja sedan. Exports grew, so a more international badge was required. This new logo featured a yellow roaring tiger's head within a green circle, mounted in a blue triangular crest topped by the word "Proton." The new badge was fine while the company was producing budget models, but as Proton started to cater for more upscale customers, a different emblem was required. Subsequently, a new badge appeared in 2008 for the launch of the second-generation Saga, which featured design input from Lotus (see pages 130–131). The new Proton symbol was now in a more stylish black and silver, with the garish colors removed. By 2016, the badge had been modernized and simplified again, with added three-dimensional shading on the tiger's head and the loss of the word "Proton." The latest badge lent a more dignified air to the new Ertiga MPV and Persona sedan.

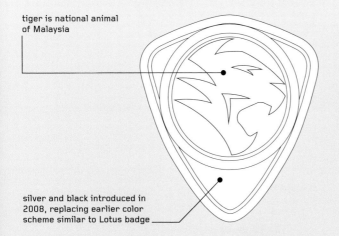

tiger is national animal of Malaysia

silver and black introduced in 2008, replacing earlier color scheme similar to Lotus badge

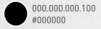

000.000.000.030
#B3B3B3

000.000.000.100
#000000

RENAULT

FOUNDED
1898 (HQ Boulogne-Billancourt, France)

FOUNDER(S)
Marcel and Fernand Renault

YEARS OF OPERATION
1899–present

BEST-KNOWN MODELS
Clio, 4, Espace, Megane, Scenic

The Renault symbol of a simple diamond has long been associated with the French manufacturer's vehicles, from the utilitarian Renault 4 of 1961 to the eccentric Twizy electric two-seater. Serious car-spotters, however, will have noted a gradual change in the diamond device. The company started using a diamond motif back in 1925, but the badge on the front of that year's Renault NN was rather different to the badge of today. The innovative, compact family car, often called the 6CV, sported a diamond bisected by rows of horizontal lines and the word "Renault" in the center. At the time, the diamond was said to represent a strong and consistent company.

Before the diamond was introduced, Renault had used a variety of badges, including one featuring the intertwined initials of the Renault brothers, who launched the company. In 1919, a logo appeared that showed an army tank in action, which reflected the company's contribution to the First World War.

Since 1925, however, all of the company's badges have been diamonds. These were gradually refined through the generations to become today's simple three-dimensional device. A key change came in 1972, when the name "Renault" was removed from the center of the diamond. That design, commissioned from the Hungarian–French artist Victor Vasarely, featured a dynamic diamond formed from a series of angular lines. Look closely at the current version and you will see that the diamond takes the form of two chevrons slightly overlapped. Another quirk to the design is the three-dimensional shading, which doesn't quite make sense.

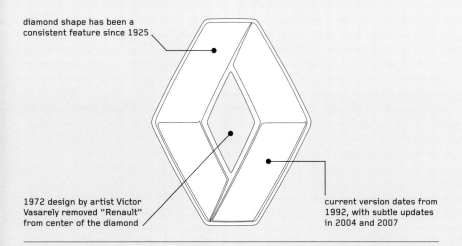

diamond shape has been a consistent feature since 1925

1972 design by artist Victor Vasarely removed "Renault" from center of the diamond

current version dates from 1992, with subtle updates in 2004 and 2007

000.000.000.030
#B3B3B3

ROLLS-ROYCE

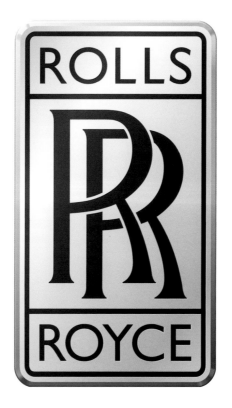

FOUNDED
1906 (Manchester, UK)

FOUNDER(S)
Henry Royce and Charles Rolls

YEARS OF OPERATION
1904–present

BEST-KNOWN MODELS
Silver Ghost, Phantom, Wraith, Corniche

Charles Rolls and Frederick Royce's luxury car-making business has earned a global reputation for peerless quality over more than 100 years, from the ten-horsepower prototypes of 1904 to today's high-tech Phantom supercars. The brand is so well known that it can boast two familiar logos. The first is an upright oblong containing two upper-case "R"s overlapping, with the words "Rolls" and "Royce" above and below. This simple badge has evolved from the partners' early flamboyant heraldic shields and crests that contained the "RR" device and plenty of decoration besides.

Besides this, Rolls-Royce has another, even more famous trademark. The "Spirit of Ecstasy" is a figure of a woman leaning forward with her arms outstretched, her dress billowing out like wings, representing "the pursuit of personal liberty, and freedom from conformity." This has been fixed to the front of every Rolls-Royce hood since the 1920s.

The romantic story behind this emblem is that the artist Charles Sykes modeled it on Eleanor Thornton, the secret lover of Lord Montagu, a motoring-mad aristocrat. His son founded the British National Motor Museum at the family home, where original models of the Spirit of Ecstasy can still be seen. Today's figure has evolved to be a little smaller and is spring-loaded for safety.

Another romantic story is that the lettering of the oblong badge was changed from red to black in 1934 to mark the death of Frederick Royce. In reality the change was simply an aesthetic choice.

intertwined double "R"
for founders Charles
Stewart Rolls and
Frederick Henry Royce

badges had red letters
prior to the 1930s

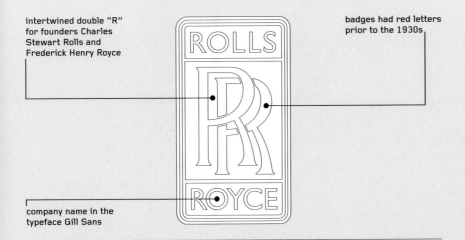

company name in the
typeface Gill Sans

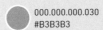 000.000.000.030
#B3B3B3

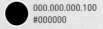 000.000.000.100
#000000

ROVER

FOUNDED
1896 (Coventry, UK)

FOUNDER(S)
J. K. Starley

YEARS OF OPERATION
1896–2005

BEST-KNOWN MODELS
Light Six, 90, 2000, Vitesse, Sterling, 75

One of the most influential British motoring brands began with the Rover 8 of 1904—a two-seater that had the unusual feature of a "backbone" rather than a chassis and no suspension at all at the back—and ended rather quietly, with the badge being laid to rest during a series of international takeovers and amalgamations. The last Rover model was the 75, an executive car, which finished production in 2005.

The fledgling company had adopted a Viking emblem as the symbol of the "rovers" of their day. At first, its bicycles and motorbcycles wore a Viking-style shield. Car badges showed a Viking warrior, then later a Viking longship figurehead. From 1922, Rover customers were offered a radiator-top figure of a Viking in a winged helmet as an extra, costing one pound.

From 1929, the Viking ship was the main emblem of the company. This was the logo on the Rover Light Six of 1930 that raced the "Blue Train" across France from Calais to Cannes as a promotional stunt. The sporty sedan won the 750-mile (1,200-kilometer) marathon by 20 minutes.

The badge evolved with the changing fortunes of the company. In the golden era of the 1950s, grand Rover sedans were driven by royalty and wore a flamboyant longboat crest. As times became tougher, the badge became simpler. Finally, it was just a graphic representation of a longboat in silver with a red sail mounted on a black plinth. The Rover brand is now the property of Tata Motors Limited, an Indian company, and for the time being has been retired from duty.

main Rover symbol was
Viking longboat

Viking figurehead
replaced earlier designs
featuring Viking warrior

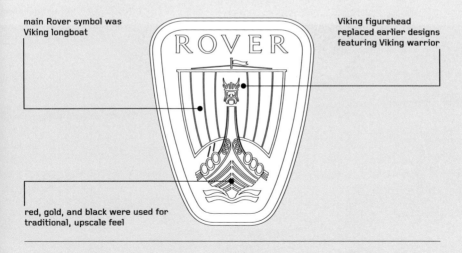

red, gold, and black were used for
traditional, upscale feel

 000.000.000.030
#B3B3B3

000.045.060.000
#FF8C66

 045.090.090.000
#8C1919

 000.000.000.100
#000000

SAAB

FOUNDED
1937 (Trollhättan, Sweden)

FOUNDER(S)
Bofors and Ab Ars (subsidiary of the Electrolux Group)

YEARS OF OPERATION
1945–2012

BEST-KNOWN MODELS
900, 99, 9-3, 9000

Since the aeronautical manufacturer Svenska Aeroplan Aktie Bolag (Swedish Airline Corporation) introduced its first car in 1947, the company acronym has gradually become more familiar than its full name. The Swedish marque became renowned for pioneering new technologies, such as turbos, pollen filters, and direct ignition. Its quirky sporty sedans, including the 99 of 1968 and the 9000 of 1984, created a cult following, particularly in the USA and UK.

Saab's advertising emphasized this quirky appeal. TV advertisements showed teams of expert drivers performing balletic formation-driving displays, or racing cars against Saab jets. In the 1980s one popular slogan was "The most intelligent cars ever built." The company badge, however, was rooted in regional tradition. The Saab factory in Trollhättan once stood in the region ruled by the Count von Skane, whose heraldic badge was a red and gold griffin, a mythical creature with the head of a hawk and the body of a lion. This constituted the emblem for the modern Swedish province of Skane, and Saab even named one of its jet fighter planes after the griffin (Gripen).

Artist Carl Fredrik Reuterswärd designed the modern combined badge (Saab and Scania) in 1984. The griffin had long been used by sister company Scania, which specializes in commercial vehicles. As the companies temporarily combined, so did the badges. The red griffin on a blue roundel survived an era of General Motors ownership. Due to financial difficulties, Saab eventually collapsed for good in 2016, while truck-maker Scania survived, along with the griffin logo.

symbol originates from
regional heraldic emblem

griffin is a mythical
creature that is half
hawk, half lion

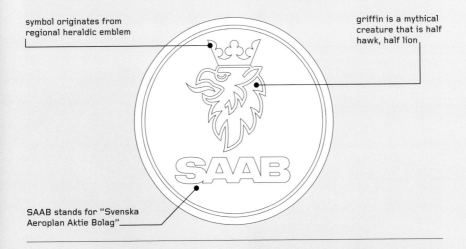

SAAB stands for "Svenska
Aeroplan Aktie Bolag"

 000.000.000.020
#CCCCCC

 020.030.080.000
#CCB333

010.100.090.000
#E60019

 100.070.000.050
#002680

SAAB: Evolution

After Saab merged with Scania, the car maker's simple name badge evolved into a joint offering with the truck builder, using the ancient symbol of a local aristocrat: the red and gold griffin.

1901

1911

1949

1954

1969

1974

1984

1995

SEAT

FOUNDED
May 9 1950, (Barcelona, Spain)

FOUNDER(S)
State government

YEARS OF OPERATION
1950–present

BEST-KNOWN MODELS
Ibiza, Leon, Toledo, Alhambra

The Spanish government established the Sociedad Espanola de Automoviles de Turismo (Spanish Touring Cars Corporation) in 1950 to kick-start the nation's motor industry following the ravages of a civil war and disruptions caused by the Second World War. The company initially produced rebranded Fiat vehicles. For example, the Seat 1400 was simply a Fiat 1400. This insignia was a red shield featuring the acronym "SEAT" in type highly reminiscent of the current Fiat logo (see page 80), with stylized chrome wings on either side.

The new company was a success among car-starved domestic buyers, and in the 1960s it expanded its range to include popular small models, such as the 800, containing a high proportion of local input. Seat even began exporting its vehicles.

By the 1970s, the company logo had also evolved, now featuring a simple use of the company name in block capitals, each in its own square of color. The badge remained similar to the Fiat emblem of the era, demonstrating the larger role that the Italian company was taking in the running of its Spanish sister company.

However, in the 1980s, the Spanish government and Fiat had a disagreement and Seat went on alone with its own logo: an "S" with a striped middle section. As Seat increasingly became part of the Volkswagen Group, this logo was refined gradually. Today, Seat is wholly owned by the German multinational, and the current badge, a chunky chrome "S" split by a dynamic diagonal stroke, has not changed significantly since the 1980s.

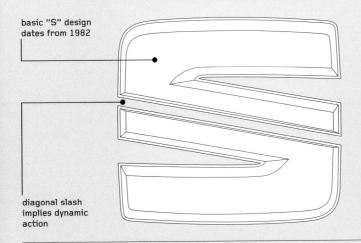

basic "S" design
dates from 1982

diagonal slash
implies dynamic
action

000.000.000.030
#B3B3B3

ŠKODA

FOUNDED
1895 (Mladá Boleslav, Czech Republic)

FOUNDER(S)
Vaclav Laurin and Vaclav Klement

YEARS OF OPERATION
1895–present

BEST-KNOWN MODELS
Rapid, Favorit, Fabia, Octavia, Superb, Yeti

One of the oldest motor manufacturers featured in this book, Škoda has been through a roller-coaster history since its origins as the 19th-century bicycle manufacturer Laurin & Klement. This company was taken over by the Czech industrial conglomerate Škoda in 1925. Cars of the era wore a simple badge featuring the script "Škoda" surrounded by a laurel wreath on a black roundel. In the 1930s, however, a new and more distinctive trademark emerged: a winged arrow featuring a circular cutout in the center that is said to resemble an eye, symbolizing the company's forward-thinking approach.

The company was taken over by the Germans during the Second World War, when it produced military hardware. It was then nationalized under the Communist government and, despite an interesting use of rear-engined configurations, Škoda's products were considered dated and often became the subject of jokes in Western countries. Following the breakup of the Soviet Union in 1991, Škoda was privatized and the quality of its manufacturing soared. The company became part of the Volkswagen Group and now the brand's quality is considered on a par with its parent company. Throughout all these upheavals, the winged arrow has remained the marque's symbol. While its symbolism may seem a bit tenuous, that little "eye-like" circle contributes to a unique insignia that has received few changes over the years, although more recently its dominant color has become green to take advantage of the fashion for environmental concerns.

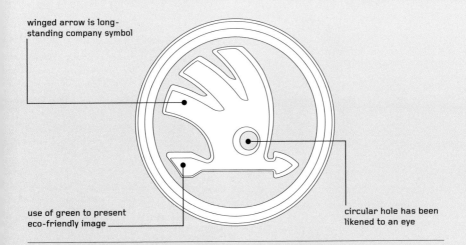

winged arrow is long-standing company symbol

use of green to present eco-friendly image

circular hole has been likened to an eye

 000.000.000.030
#B3B3B3

 085.000.100.000
#26FF00

 000.000.000.100
#000000

SMART

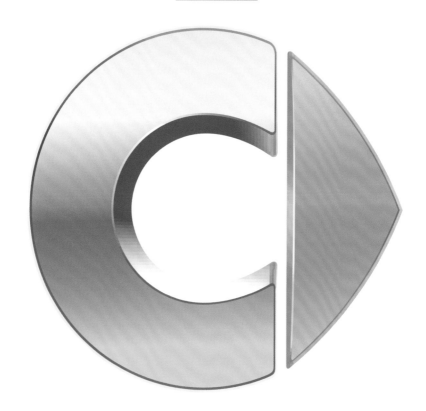

FOUNDED
1994 (Hambach, France)

FOUNDER(S)
Nicolas Hayek (Swatch) and Mercedes-Benz

YEARS OF OPERATION
1994–present

BEST-KNOWN MODELS
Fortwo, Forfour

Four years after the company was founded, everything about the launch of the Smart car in 1998 was extraordinary. Here was a futuristic micro-car that could park end-on to the sidewalk and promised to ease urban congestion. The tiny two-seater was sold from glass "Smart towers" that resembled vending machines. In some countries, the cars were available to buy from department stores. In total, more than a million cars were sold in the company's first decade. Since then, the Smart range has expanded into tiny sports cars, four-seaters, and all-electric models.

The new brand was an offshoot of the long-standing traditional German company Mercedes, but it was its association with Swatch watches that gave these cars all the style and marketing expertise available.

The marque was officially called "smart" in simple lower-case letters and the original two-seater was called the Fortwo. The Smart logo at the front of every vehicle was similarly simple and modern: a chrome circle with a built-in yellow arrow. The emblem resembles the power button on modern technological devices. The design forms a letter "C" for "compact" and the right-pointing arrow resembles "forward thinking."

Long hours of clever graphic design helped establish this successful and innovative new brand. Smart marketing chiefs were dismayed, however, to discover that many owners preferred to prize off the slick Smart badge and replace it with the prestigious logo of its parent company, Mercedes (see pages 140–143).

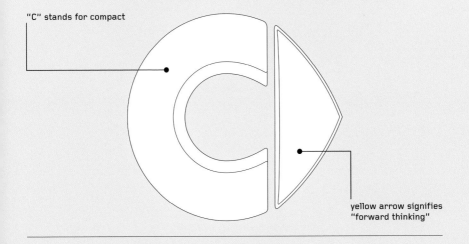

"C" stands for compact

yellow arrow signifies
"forward thinking"

000.000.000.030
#B3B3B3

015.030.100.000
#D9B300

SSANGYONG

FOUNDED
1954 (Seoul, South Korea)

FOUNDER(S)
State government

YEARS OF OPERATION
1954–present

BEST-KNOWN MODELS
Musso, Korando, Rexton, Chairman

SsangYong, which means "double dragons" in Korean, may have become a subdivision of Indian-based conglomerate Mahindra (see pages 132–133), but it has been allowed to retain its own distinct identity, including its distinctive badge.

The South Korean manufacturer has endured a short but muddled and turbulent history. The small factory of the Dong-A Motor Company was already building military and commercial vehicles when it was taken over by an industrial group called SsangYong in the mid 1980s. This led to the birth of a new motoring brand. In the early 1990s, SsangYong began a joint project with Mercedes to build the Musso SUV. With manufacturers from the Far East apparently conquering much of the global market, things looked promising for the fledgling Korean company. However, the fortunes of SsangYong were soon beset by financial difficulties and it was involved in a brief, unsuccessful alliance with General Motors and Daewoo.

The final takeover by Indian company Mahindra in 2011 appears to have steadied SsangYong's business. The marque now produces a full range of vehicles, from the Actyon Sports pickup truck to the Chairman luxury sedan. All these vehicles wear the SsangYong badge. At first glance, this appears to be a simple circular, symmetrical graphic symbol. The company, however, explains that the design in fact represents the two dragons of its name, with their wings rising upward toward heaven.

graphic device represents
two dragons intertwined

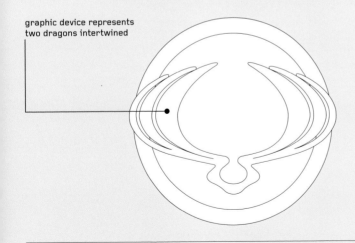

000.000.000.030
#B3B3B3

000.000.000.100
#000000

SUBARU

FOUNDED
1953 (Tokyo, Japan)

FOUNDER(S)
Fuji Kogyo, Fuji Jidosha, Omiya Fuji Kogyo,
Utsunomiya Sharyo, and Tokyo Fuji Sangyo

YEARS OF OPERATION
1954–present

BEST-KNOWN MODELS
Legacy, Impreza, Forester

The Japanese industrial group Fuji Heavy Industries Ltd. was formed in 1953 when five different engineering operations merged. First, the new company chose a friendlier trading name as their car marque: Subaru. This is the Japanese name for a constellation that is known elsewhere as the Pleiades or "The Seven Sisters."

The next job was to establish a car-making division. This was less easy to achieve. The first car was proudly named the Subaru 1500, which was released in 1954 as a prototype and the company produced only 20 of them. The insignia for the cars seemed a straightforward choice, however. Subaru chose an arrangement of the stars showing the constellation from which it took its name. Eagle-eyed car-spotters will notice that this badge features six stars, but this is not an oversight: the

constellation does indeed comprise seven stars, but one of them is so close to another that it is invisible to the naked eye.

Meanwhile, Subaru started honing its identity with the distinctive boxer engine, which appeared in the 1000 model in 1965, and the four-wheel-drive systems that appeared in the Brat pickup from 1977 as well as later cars, including the Impreza and Legacy.

As the company grew into a global success, the logo evolved. One of the stars on the badge was made larger, to signify the creation of Fuji Heavy Industries Ltd. from the group of five other companies. The badge has been subtly smartened to suit Subaru's affluent discerning customer base, and the chrome, three-dimensional stars now sit on a deep blue oval within a silver frame.

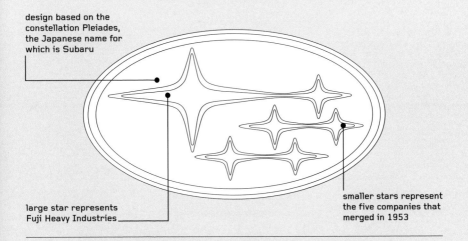

design based on the constellation Pleiades, the Japanese name for which is Subaru

large star represents Fuji Heavy Industries

smaller stars represent the five companies that merged in 1953

000.000.000.030
#B3B3B3

100.070.000.020
#003DCC

SUZUKI

FOUNDED
1909 (Hamamatsu, Japan.)

FOUNDER(S)
Michio Suzuki

YEARS OF OPERATION
1909–present

BEST-KNOWN MODELS
LJ series, SJ Series, Vitara, Swift, Jimny

Michio Suzuki founded a company in 1909 that for 30 years concentrated on making cloth-weaving machines. As Japan recovered from the ravages of the Second World War, Suzuki began making motorized bicycles and, by 1955, its first production car. The mechanical sophistication of the Suzulight sedan was way ahead of its time—but it was sold under its own name, not Suzuki. The company did not establish an automotive division until 1961 but, even then, the light vans it built were still branded Suzulight.

Suzuki motorcycles were already successful across the globe when a simple, small off-roader became the breakthrough model for Suzuki's automotive marque. The LJ10 light jeep, known as the "Jimny," "Stockman," or "Eljot" in some markets, was a three-seater, convertible off-roader with a tiny engine. It was, however, a big sales success, and began a tradition of small Suzuki jeeps that has continued through the SJ series to today's Jimny models.

Today Suzuki is a brand encompassing all sorts of engineering products. Its auto division is one of Japan's most successful. Suzuki vehicles range from off-roaders to sporty hatchbacks, and their emblem is, like the company, unpretentious. The typeface suggests three short brushstrokes, perhaps hinting at Japanese calligraphy. It's a simple but effective initial logo that has been almost unchanged since it was introduced in 1958 and today appears on a wide range of cars, vans, motorcycles, engines, and engineering products produced by the company. Unlike Honda (see pages 98–99), Suzuki uses the same badge for both its cars and its motorbikes.

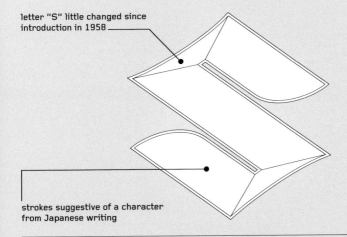

letter "S" little changed since introduction in 1958

strokes suggestive of a character from Japanese writing

000.000.000.030
#B3B3B3

TATA

FOUNDED
1945

FOUNDER(S)
Jamsetji Nusserwanji Tata

YEARS OF OPERATION
1954–present

BEST-KNOWN MODELS
Sierra, Nano, Indica

Pioneering industrialist Jamsetji Nusserwanji Tata established a large group of companies across India 150 years ago. His company, formerly known as Tata Engineering and Locomotive Company, grew to become the subcontinent's largest multinational conglomerate. Tata Motors was launched in 1945 but didn't start making vehicles until 1954, and that was a collaborative van-building project jointly operated with Daimler-Benz. Making passenger cars didn't begin until 1991, with the launch of the Tata Sierra SUV based on the Group's popular TL pickup.

This first production car carried the badge that has since become familiar as the Tata emblem. It was also seen on the front grille of the Tata Indica, a supermini launched in 1998, known as the first passenger vehicle to be produced in India.

The badge itself is superficially simple: an oval containing an upper-case letter "T." The design sophistication is that the "T" is split vertically, which allows it to have other graphic interpretations, too. To some, it symbolizes a "fountain of knowledge," a "tree of trust," or even a straight road heading to the horizon. Today, the badge can be seen on cars, buses, and trucks everywhere in India.

The company now produces a range of popular vehicles under its own name, such as the Nano city car, often referred to as the world's cheapest car, the Hexa SUV, and the Zest family sedan. The Tata Group has also taken over well-known international motoring marques, including Jaguar Land Rover (see pages 108–109 and 124–125) and Daewoo (see pages 64–65).

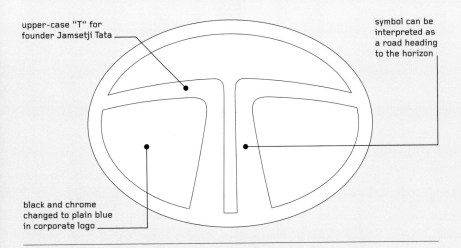

upper-case "T" for founder Jamsetji Tata

symbol can be interpreted as a road heading to the horizon

black and chrome changed to plain blue in corporate logo

000.000.000.030
#B3B3B3

000.000.000.100
#000000

TESLA

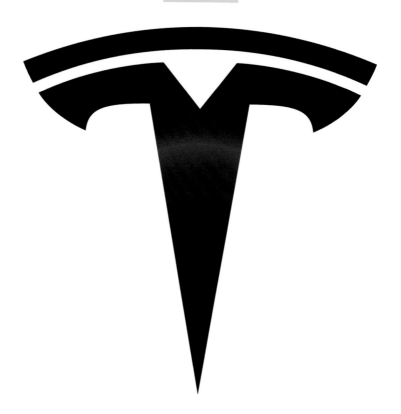

FOUNDED
2003 (Menlo Park, California, USA)

FOUNDER(S)
Martin Eberhard and Marc Tarpenning

YEARS OF OPERATION
2003–present

BEST-KNOWN MODELS
Roadster, Model S

Tesla first received global headlines with the release of the Roadster in 2008. The exciting new vehicle was the world's first mass-produced electric sports car. Its successor, the elegant and sporty Model S, arrived just four years later and has gone on to become one of the world's best-selling electric cars.

Since then, Tesla has repeatedly stepped ahead of much of the rest in the motor industry, unveiling products such as the Model X, an electric SUV, and, most recently, the Model 3, an affordable, electric, luxury family car that is tipped to be the landmark car for the digital generation. Tesla has also invested in a network of dedicated "supercharging" points across North America, Europe, and parts of Asia.

Other divisions of the company are also heavily involved in developing alternative energy products and solutions in a wide range of applications, from high-capacity batteries to solar roof tiles.

The company has an overall logo that is used as an emblem on all products. Tesla's cars wear it as a prominent badge on their front end. At first, this looks like a simple capital "T," obviously standing for "Tesla." The emblem was, however, created by acclaimed New Jersey designers RO Studio, and Tesla CEO ElonMusk claims the symbol is a lot more sophisticated than a basic initial. The badge is, he says, both a letter "T" and a cross-section of part of an electric motor.

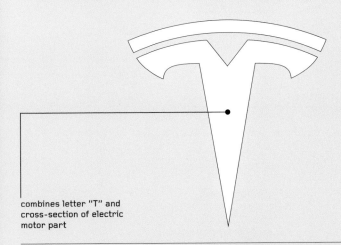

combines letter "T" and
cross-section of electric
motor part

000.000.000.030
#B3B3B3

000.000.000.100
#000000

TOYOTA

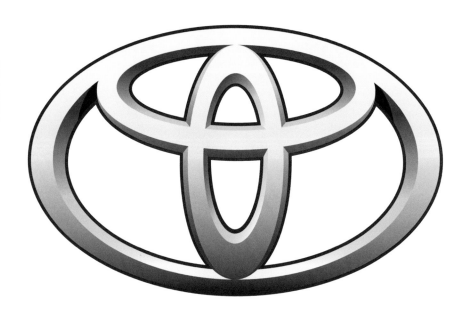

FOUNDED
1937 (Nagoya, Japan).

FOUNDER(S)
Sakichi, Risaburo, and Kiichiro Toyoda

YEARS OF OPERATION
1937–present

BEST-KNOWN MODELS
Corolla, Camry, Land Cruiser, MR2, Celica

In 1936, a competition was held to design a new logo for a rapidly growing Japanese car manufacturer. Until then, its logo had featured the founder's family name—Toyoda—in upper-case letters. The winning entry used the Japanese characters for "to," "yo," and "ta," and as a result the company name was changed to Toyota. This was partly for design reasons, and reportedly also because in Japan the number eight is auspicious (it takes eight strokes to draw the logo if the third character is "ta," but ten strokes if it is "da").

The symbol we recognize today was adopted in 1989 to commemorate the company's 50th anniversary, and also to create an individual international identity distinct from its new luxury marque, Lexus (see pages 126–127). The design took five years and featured three interlocking ovals,

positioned with a vertical line of symmetry. The ovals form a letter "T." They also represent a mutually beneficial relationship between the company and its customers, with the external oval signifying the world embracing this international company. The varying thickness of the lines used hints at traditional Japanese calligraphy.

The company soon introduced its new symbol across its worldwide organization, including signage for showrooms, printed material, and, of course, the cars themselves. The first car to wear the new badge was the Toyota Celsior in Japan. Confusingly, the vehicle was called the Lexus LS everywhere else—and it wore a Lexus badge instead. Since then, however, generations of Toyotas have used the new badge, which has barely changed since its introduction.

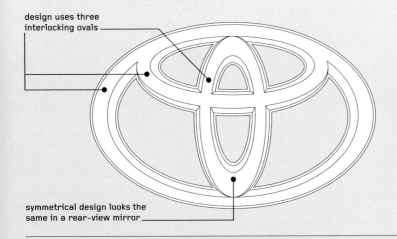

design uses three
interlocking ovals

symmetrical design looks the
same in a rear-view mirror

TRIUMPH

FOUNDED
1885 (London, UK)

FOUNDER(S)
Siegfried Bettmann

YEARS OF OPERATION
1889–1984

BEST-KNOWN MODELS
TR6, TR7, Herald, Stag, Dolomite

One of the UK's classic marques was founded by German immigrant Siegfried Bettmann. The former sewing machine salesman started making bicycles, then motorcycles, and finally cars in 1921. The elegant 10/20 was Triumph's first four-wheeler, followed by the Super Seven. In 1936, financial difficulties led to the car and motorcycle businesses being separated. Triumph cars of this era were distinguished by a badge featuring the company name written across a blue and red globe.

Triumph was bought by the Standard Motor Company in 1944 and the subsidiary company evolved into a sportier brand. Cars were badged with globes, winged motifs, or the striped shield of Standard. The TR series of sports cars started its 30-year run, ending with the TR8 in 1981.

By the 1980s, Triumph had become assimilated into the British Leyland empire. The cars were given hood badges that were simply the company name in capital letters. The stylish Stag convertible wore a special stag badge and later Triumphs received a new emblem: the Triumph name surrounded by a laurel wreath on a black roundel.

All this badge tinkering failed to save the marque, however. Its last model was the Acclaim sedan, which was a Honda Ballade remarketed with a Triumph badge. Finally, in 1984 the shrinking Austin Rover Group retired the Triumph marque. The name came into the hands of BMW in 1994 when it bought the Rover Group, although it hasn't appeared on a car since this time.

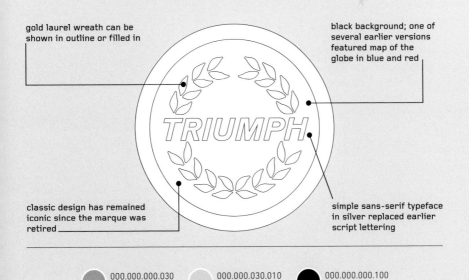

gold laurel wreath can be shown in outline or filled in

black background; one of several earlier versions featured map of the globe in blue and red

classic design has remained iconic since the marque was retired

simple sans-serif typeface in silver replaced earlier script lettering

000.000.000.030
#B3B3B3

000.000.030.010
#E6E6A1

000.000.000.100
#000000

TVR

FOUNDED
1947 (Blackpool, UK)

FOUNDER(S)
Trevor Wilkinson

YEARS OF OPERATION
1947–present

BEST-KNOWN MODELS
Griffith, Tuscan, Chimaera

British businessman Trevor Wilkinson established mechanical engineering company TVR Engineering in 1947, using the consonants of his first name. He began building specialist sports cars in the years following, and by 1953 TVR was offering a sports sedan in a kit form. It sported a smart new logo designed by Wilkinson's friend, art student John Cookson.

TVR gradually grew in confidence and ambition, eventually producing a range of high-performance sports cars. TVR products were characterized by the use of lightweight bodies, rear-wheel drive, and powerful engines from other manufacturers. The Griffith of 1963, for example, used a Ford V8 in a fiberglass body to achieve 0–60 mph (0–96 kph) in less than four seconds, an astonishing acceleration for this era.

The small company veered from one financial crisis to the next and acquired a sequence of owners. Now, eventually, it appears to have found stability in the hands of Les Edgar, who bought the company in 2013. Plans for a new factory were announced in 2016, along with plans for an exciting carbon-fiber sports car powered by a Cosworth V8. Throughout these turbulent times the cars have continued in the high-performance tradition of the marque. They also still wear the simple TVR logo designed in the 1950s. This badge shows an overlapping arrangement of the three letters of the name in block capitals. Cleverly, the letters are filled with horizontal lines that are designed to suggest the central "V" also has two wings extending from either side.

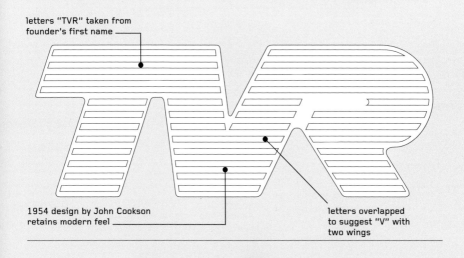

letters "TVR" taken from founder's first name

1954 design by John Cookson retains modern feel

letters overlapped to suggest "V" with two wings

000.000.000.030
#B3B3B3

000.000.000.080
#333333

VAUXHALL

FOUNDED
1857 (London, UK)

FOUNDER(S)
Alexander Wilson

YEARS OF OPERATION
1857–present

BEST-KNOWN MODELS
Victor, Viva, Cavalier, Astra, Corsa, Zafira

Sir Falkes de Breauté was a powerful Norman mercenary soldier during the reign of King John, 800 years ago. The heraldic device on his pennants and shields was the griffin— the same mythical beast, half eagle, half lion, that appeared on the Saab badge (see pages 182–185). The knight had been granted the manor of Luton, to the north of London, and had a home in London called Falkes' Hall. Over the years, this evolved into Vauxhall, now a district of south London.

The Vauxhall car company originated in that southern area of London, under the name Vauxhall Ironworks. Because of Vauxhall's historical associations with de Breauté, the company chose to use the griffin as its trademark. In 1905, the Vauxhall car company moved north, to de Breauté's manor of Luton. The marque badge continued and has done for more than 100 years to the present day, in honor of Sir Falkes.

Today, the badge is certainly better known than the Norman soldier-turned knight. In fact, it has adorned Vauxhall vehicles since the first model appeared in 1903, which had a tiller instead of a steering wheel. At first Vauxhall was a luxury brand, but after it was taken over by General Motors (GM) in 1925 the marque began to concentrate on mass-market models. After the Second World War the Vauxhall range became very closely linked to the fellow GM brand of Opel (see pages 160–161). Today it has a wide range of popular models, from the Adam city car to the Zafira people-carrier, and they all still wear the traditional Vauxhall griffin badge.

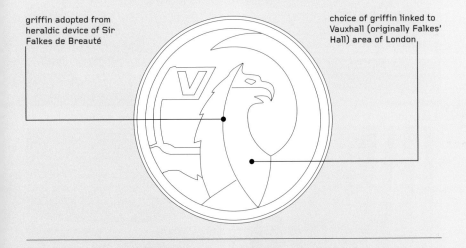

griffin adopted from heraldic device of Sir Falkes de Breauté

choice of griffin linked to Vauxhall (originally Falkes' Hall) area of London

000.000.000.030
#B3B3B3

000.100.100.000
#FF0000

VAUXHALL: Evolution

The griffin appeared in the early days of Vauxhall cars. Since then the historic heraldic beast has been refined as design tastes change, eventually becoming today's simple graphic logo.

1914

1920s

1920s

1920s

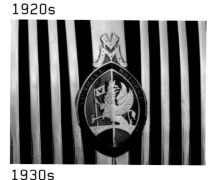

1930s

1946

1960s

1968

1970s

1978

1996

2003

VOLKSWAGEN

FOUNDED
May 28 1937 (Wolfsburg, Germany)

FOUNDER(S)
State government

YEARS OF OPERATION
1937–present

BEST-KNOWN MODELS
Beetle, Golf, Polo, Campervan

The idea of a *Volks Wagen* ("people's car") originates in pre-Second World War Germany. Designer Ferdinand Porsche came up with the plan for the rear-engined, rounded shape that eventually became the Beetle. Production of this vehicle was started properly in war-torn Germany during the British occupation, and the Volkswagen (VW) name was formally adopted. Sales grew rapidly, exports began, and the company's second model, the VW Campervan, was another big success.

These vehicles went out into the world wearing a simple badge that has become one of the most famous in the automotive industry. The design features a "V" over a "W" within a circle. The exact designer responsible for this letter arrangement has been the subject of legal disputes, with possibilities including artist Martin Freyer and Porsche employee Franz Reimspiess. Originally the circle around the emblem appeared like a cog, but after the war it was simplified. Except for a switch from black to blue in 1967, the badge has remained much the same ever since.

As the appeal of the Beetle declined in the 1970s, VW came up with another massive worldwide sales success, the Golf. This family hatchback has remained a major part of VW's range. The company has continued to grow, releasing a wide range of vehicles from city cars, such as the Lupo, to luxury sedans, such as the Phaeton, and from sports cars, including the Scirocco, to SUVs like the T-Roc. VW has also taken over a swathe of other manufacturers, including Audi and Škoda, so that it now stands at the head of one of the world's largest auto manufacturing groups.

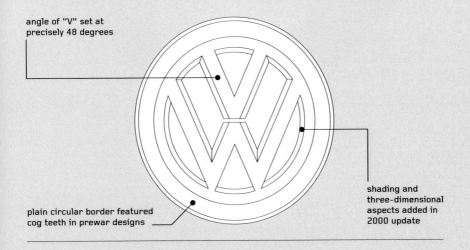

angle of "V" set at
precisely 48 degrees

plain circular border featured
cog teeth in prewar designs

shading and
three-dimensional
aspects added in
2000 update

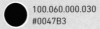

000.000.000.030
#B3B3B3

100.060.000.030
#0047B3

VOLVO

FOUNDED
1926 (Gothenburg, Sweden)

FOUNDER(S)
Assar Gabrielsson and Gustaf Larsson

YEARS OF OPERATION
1927–present

BEST-KNOWN MODELS
XC90, Amazon, V70, P1800

When Swedish manufacturing company Svenska Kullagerfabriken decided to start producing cars in 1926, they reactivated an old company with a very distinct name. Several words, in various languages, derive from the infinitive form of the Latin verb *volvere*, but they all, in one way or another, describe a rotating movement; for example, "revolve" in English. The far-sighted financiers behind the launch of Volvo also came up with a logo. They used the ancient chemical symbol for iron: a circle with a diagonal arrow. The Romans used this symbol for Mars, the god of war, which also represents the male gender.

The first cars, the large open-top ÖV4, often referred to as the "Jakob," appeared with this symbol on the front grille, combined with a diagonal band to hold the badge in place. When the designers registered the logo they simply took a picture of the entire radiator grille and registered the lot. As a result, that diagonal band has also become a Volvo trademark.

This strong, masculine branding served the new company well, and the badge has evolved only slightly since then. It now features the word "Volvo" in a band across the center (the company name was originally displayed on a separate badge) and features three-dimensional shading. The symbol is usually featured on all Volvo car and truck steering wheels, as well as on wheel hubs. The original, rather macho image of the "iron" company has softened considerably. Volvo is now as famous for safety and environmentalism as it is for sturdy, reliable vehicles.

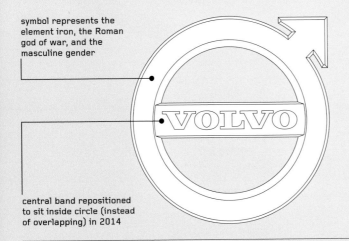

symbol represents the element iron, the Roman god of war, and the masculine gender

central band repositioned to sit inside circle (instead of overlapping) in 2014

000.000.000.030
#B3B3B3

100.085.000.015
#0021D9

ZAZ

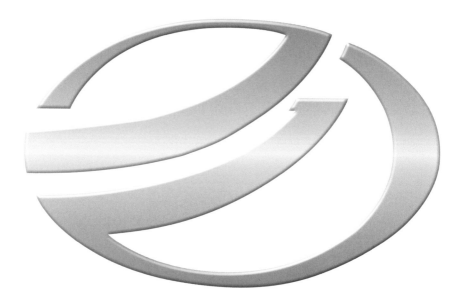

FOUNDED
1863 (Zaporizhia, Ukraine)

FOUNDER(S)
Abraham Koop

YEARS OF OPERATION
1863–present

BEST-KNOWN MODELS
Zaporozhets, Lanos, Vida

Zaporizhia Automobile Building Plant was established in the mid 1800s for the production of agricultural machines and equipment. The company changed its name to ZAZ in 1959 with the advent of its first passenger car, and the stage was set for the start of the Ukrainian motor industry.

The first Zaporozhet rear-wheel-drive supermini rolled off the production line in the city of Zaporizhia in southeastern Ukraine. This rear-engined "Soviet Beetle" was a crude copy of a Fiat 600 with some local adaptations, so it wore a small red pentagonal badge featuring the new ZAZ name. The Zaporozhets continued in production until 1994. The quirky little vehicles had a bad reputation across the USSR, but they acquired a cult following that continues today.

After the breakup of the Soviet Union in the 1998, ZAZ made an alliance with Daewoo (see pages 64–65), assembling the more modern Korean models in Ukraine. ZAZ also made agreements with manufacturers such as Chery, Kia (see pages 112–113), and Chevrolet (see pages 52–53) to build their cars. Today ZAZ assembles vehicles for a variety of foreign marques. All this helped modernize the local car industry until successful domestic cars, including the Sens and Vida, could be produced alongside them. These cars are fitted with the ZAZ badge, which has evolved to become as modern-looking as the cars. It is a chrome oval bisected by two thick sweeping lines. It could be a simple graphic device—or it could represent a road curving away appealingly into the horizon.

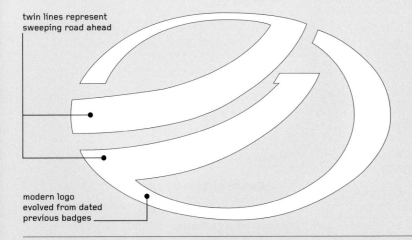

twin lines represent
sweeping road ahead

modern logo
evolved from dated
previous badges

000.000.000.030
#B3B3B3

ZiL

FOUNDED
1916 (Moscow, Russia)

FOUNDER(S)
State government

YEARS OF OPERATION
1924–2012

BEST-KNOWN MODELS
ZIS-101, 41041

Some main roads in Moscow feature a special lane for senior government officials to drive along without being hindered by normal traffic. Locals call these "ZiL lanes." For example, on Kutuzovsky Prospekt the ZiL lane runs right down the middle of the multilane highway. "ZiL" is an acronym that stands for Zavod Imeni Likhachova, the Likhachov factory in Moscow that was a major manufacturer of military vehicles, buses, trucks, and luxury cars for the political elite.

The factory had been founded just before the Revolution of 1916, but it took eight years of upheaval before it built its first vehicle, which was a truck. The marque really made its name, however, by producing armored limousines for Soviet leaders. Cars ranged from the 1½-gallon prewar ZIS-101 used by Stalin, to the 41041 open-top model used in May Day parades in Red Square until the early part of the 21st century. The 2-gallon ZiL-4104 of the 1970s had one of the world's biggest passenger-car engines. Only a few dozen ZiL cars were produced annually. These had prices equivalent to Rolls-Royces (see pages 178–179), but lacked the matching engineering finesse.

The brand's badges seem mysterious to non-Russian speakers, but simply represent the company initials in the Cyrillic alphabet. These initials are usually portrayed against a rectangular frame, either as a blue badge or as a mascot mounted on top of the hood.

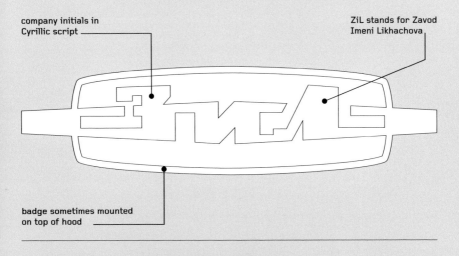

company initials in
Cyrillic script

ZiL stands for Zavod
Imeni Likhachova

badge sometimes mounted
on top of hood

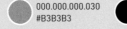 000.000.000.030
#B3B3B3

 000.000.000.100
#000000

INDEX

CREDITS

Picture Credits

Trade Marks